Ladies' Home Journal®

100 GREAT

CHICKEN

RECIPES

LADIES' HOME JOURNAL™ BOOKS
New York/Des Moines

LADIES' HOME JOURNAL™ BOOKS
An Imprint of Meredith® Books
President, Book Group: Joseph J. Ward
Vice President and Editorial Director: Elizabeth P. Rice
Art Director: Ernest Shelton

LADIES' HOME JOURNAL®
Publishing Director and Editor-in-Chief: Myrna Blyth
Food Editor: Jan Turner Hazard
Associate Food Editors: Susan Sarao Westmoreland, Lisa Brainerd

100 GREAT CHICKEN RECIPES
Project Manager/ Editor: Shelli McConnell
Writer/ Researcher: Carol Prager
Graphic Designers: Jeff Harrison, Tom Wegner
Food Stylist: Rick Ellis
Prop Stylist: Bette Blau
Photographer: Corinne Colen Photography
Production Manager: Doug Johnston
Graphic Production Coordinator: Paula Forest

On the cover: Roast Chicken with 20 Cloves of Garlic, page 21.

Meredith Corporation Corporate Officers
Chairman of the Executive Committee: E. T. Meredith III
Chairman of the Board, President and Chief Executive Officer: Jack D. Rehm
Group Presidents: Joseph J. Ward, Books; William T. Kerr, Magazines;
Philip A. Jones, Broadcasting; Allen L. Sabbag, Real Estate
Vice Presidents: Leo R. Armatis, Corporate Relations; Thomas G. Fisher, General Counsel
and Secretary; Larry D. Hartsook, Finance; Michael A. Sell, Treasurer; Kathleen J. Zehr,
Controller and Assistant Secretary

We Care!
All of us at Ladies' Home Journal™ Books are dedicated to providing you with the ideas and
recipe information you need to create wonderful foods. We welcome your comments and
suggestions. Write us at: Ladies' Home Journal™ Books, Cookbook Editorial Department,
RW-240, 1716 Locust St., Des Moines, IA 50309-3023.

If you would like to order additional copies of any of our books, call 1-800-678-2803.

To ensure that Ladies' Home Journal® recipes
meet the highest standards for flavor, nutrition,
appearance and reliability, we test them a
minimum of three times in our own kitchen.
That makes for quality you can count on.

Chicken—It's Everyone's Favorite

The popularity of chicken is no secret. Everybody knows it's quick, inexpensive, and good for you. Versatility is what makes chicken truly amazing. However you cook it—flamed on the grill until tender and smoky, stir-fried in minutes, or simmered in a comforting stew—chicken is always right at home. Chicken's subtle taste is also the perfect complement for an infinite number of flavors. It is easily paired with the hottest of sauces or tossed in a cool, refreshing salad. So here's our collection of recipes just for cooking chicken, a practically perfect bird.

CONTENTS

Down-Home Chicken Classics

Good ol' comfort food at its finest—brimful potpies, savory stews, and crispy fried chicken.

6

Chicken Spans the Globe

Chicken's fare in cuisines from across the world.

26

Chicken from the Border

A round-up of favorite burritos, enchiladas, tamales, and more.

62

Chicken Good and Quick

Fabulous recipes that are long on flavor when you're short on time—ready in 30 minutes, start to finish.

80

Chicken with Crunch

Choice chicken specialties that are crunchy on the outside and juicy on the inside.

106

Chicken in a Salad Bowl

Delicious main-dish salads whether they're cold, hot, tossed, arraranged, casual, or elegant.

118

Chicken with Fire and Smoke

Sizzling specialties for the grill that are marinated, sauced, or basted.

130

Index

142

DOWN-HOME

CHICKEN CLASSICS

Comfort comes to mind when we think of a chicken in every pot and here's a selection of roasts, potpies and stews that will bring the flavor of Sunday supper to your table any night of the week! So get cozy with warm and nostalgic Chicken and Cornmeal Dumplings, Roast Herb Chicken with Barley Stuffing or Brunswick Stew and celebrate these all-time favorites that could only be made in the USA.

BUFFALO CHICKEN WINGS

This zesty chicken appetizer, now a favorite from coast to coast, originated at the Anchor Bar in Buffalo, New York. No need for frying in this version, the wings are roasted on a rack to extra-crisp perfection.

Prep time: 20 minutes plus chilling
Cooking time: 45 minutes
○ *Degree of difficulty: easy*

- 24 **chicken wings (about 4 pounds), tips trimmed**
- 2 **tablespoons butter *or* margarine, melted**
- 4 **to 5 tablespoons hot red pepper sauce**
- 2 **teaspoons cider vinegar**
  Celery sticks

Blue Cheese Dip

- ½ **cup sour cream**
- ½ **cup mayonnaise**
- 2 **ounces blue cheese, crumbled**
- 1 **green onion, sliced thin**

- ½ **teaspoon minced garlic**
- ¼ **teaspoon salt**
- ¼ **teaspoon freshly ground pepper**

1 Preheat oven to 450° F. Cut each wing into 2 pieces at the joint. Arrange the wing pieces in a single layer on a flat rack placed in a roasting pan.

2 Combine the butter, hot sauce, and vinegar in a small bowl. Brush half the sauce on the wing pieces.

3 Roast the wing pieces for 25 minutes. Brush remaining sauce on wing pieces. Roast for 20 minutes more. Serve with celery sticks and Blue Cheese Dip. Makes 8 servings.

Blue Cheese Dip: Combine all ingredients in a medium bowl. Refrigerate at least 1 hour. Makes 1¼ cups.

PER SERVING WITH DIP		DAILY GOAL
Calories	430	2,000 (F), 2,500 (M)
Total Fat	35 g	60 g or less (F), 70 g or less (M)
Saturated fat	11 g	20 g or less (F), 23 g or less (M)
Cholesterol	100 mg	300 mg or less
Sodium	573 mg	2,400 mg or less
Carbohydrates	1 g	250 g or more
Protein	25 g	55 g to 90 g

NOTES

DOWN-HOME CHICKEN AND BISCUITS

We've trimmed the fat but not a bit of flavor from this luscious casserole which features a cornucopia of vegetables and a tender buttermilk biscuit topping.

▼ *Low-fat*
▽ *Low-calorie*
   Prep time: 30 minutes
   Baking time: 12 to 15 minutes
○ *Degree of difficulty: easy*

1   can (13¾ *or* 14½ ounces) chicken broth, plus enough water to equal 3 cups
1   pound boneless, skinless chicken breasts
1   cup thick-sliced carrots
2   cups diced yellow squash
1   cup trimmed, halved green beans
½   cup chopped green onions
3   tablespoons cornstarch
1   cup skim milk, divided
½   teaspoon dillweed
½   teaspoon salt
⅛   teaspoon freshly ground pepper
    Pinch thyme
1   cup frozen peas

Biscuits
1   cup all-purpose flour
1   teaspoon baking powder
¼   teaspoon baking soda
¼   teaspoon salt
2   tablespoons vegetable shortening
½   cup low-fat buttermilk

1   Bring the chicken broth and water to a boil in a large saucepan over medium heat. Add the chicken; cover and simmer for 10 minutes. With a slotted spoon, transfer chicken to a plate.

2   Add the carrots to the saucepan and cook for 7 minutes. Add the squash, green beans, and green onions; cook for 2 minutes more. With a slotted spoon, transfer vegetables to the plate.

3   Heat broth over medium-low heat for 1 minute. Stir the cornstarch into ¼ cup of the milk until smooth. Whisk cornstarch mixture into broth, along with the remaining milk, dillweed, salt, pepper, and thyme. Bring to a boil. Reduce heat and simmer for 2 minutes.

4   Cut the chicken into bite-size pieces. Stir chicken, cooked vegetables, and peas into the sauce and cook until heated through. Transfer to a warm, shallow 2-quart casserole. Top with biscuits and serve immediately. Makes 6 servings.

Biscuits: Preheat oven to 425°F. Lightly coat a baking sheet with vegetable cooking spray. Set aside. Combine the flour, baking powder, baking soda and salt in a large bowl. With a pastry blender or 2 knives, cut in the shortening until the mixture resembles coarse crumbs. Stir in the buttermilk just until dough holds together. Drop by tablespoonfuls onto prepared baking sheet. Bake for 12 to 15 minutes until the biscuits are golden. Makes 1 dozen.

PER SERVING WITH 2 BISCUITS		DAILY GOAL
Calories	290	2,000 (F), 2,500 (M)
Total Fat	7 g	60 g or less (F), 70 g or less (M)
Saturated fat	2 g	20 g or less (F), 23 g or less (M)
Cholesterol	46 mg	300 mg or less
Sodium	848 mg	2,400 mg or less
Carbohydrates	32 g	250 g or more
Protein	24 g	55 g to 90 g

CHICKEN AND CORNMEAL DUMPLINGS

This rich chicken and broth can be prepared a day ahead, covered, and refrigerated. To skim the fat from the chilled broth, simply spoon it off the top. *Also pictured on page 6.*

▼ *Low-fat*
  Prep time: 50 minutes
  Cooking time: 30 minutes
● *Degree of difficulty: moderate*

1 **chicken (3 pounds), cut up**
1 **can (13¾ *or* 14½ ounces) chicken broth**
2 **cups water**
1 **onion, quartered**
½ **bay leaf**
½ **teaspoon thyme**
¼ **cup butter *or* margarine**
1 **cup finely chopped onions**
⅓ **cup all-purpose flour**
1 **cup milk**
1 **teaspoon salt**
½ **teaspoon freshly ground pepper**

1½ **cups thinly sliced carrots**
1 **package (10 ounces) frozen peas, thawed**
1 **package (10 ounces) frozen whole kernel corn, thawed**

Dumplings
½ **cup all-purpose flour**
½ **cup yellow cornmeal**
1½ **teaspoons baking powder**
½ **teaspoon salt**
⅛ **teaspoon ground red pepper**
⅓ **cup milk**
1 **large egg, beaten**
2 **tablespoons chopped fresh parsley**
2 **tablespoon chopped green onions**

1 Combine the chicken broth, water, onion, bay leaf, and thyme in a Dutch oven. Bring to a boil. Reduce heat and simmer for 30 minutes. Remove chicken and cool slightly. Discard the skin and bones and cut the meat into 1-inch pieces.

2 Meanwhile, strain the broth and discard any solids. (Can be made ahead. Cover and refrigerate chicken meat and broth separately up to 24 hours.) Skim fat from broth. Return broth to Dutch oven and cook over high heat until reduced to 2 cups, about 10 minutes. Remove broth from the heat and from the pot; set aside.

3 Melt the butter in the same pot over medium heat. Add the onions and cook until translucent, about 5 minutes. Stir in the flour and cook for 1 minute. Whisk in the broth, milk, salt and pepper. Bring to a boil, whisking.

4 Add the chicken, carrots, peas and corn. Return to a boil. Drop the dumpling batter on the boiling liquid by spoonfuls and simmer, covered, for 10 minutes, then uncovered for 10 minutes more. Makes 6 servings.

Dumplings: Stir the flour, cornmeal, baking powder, salt and red pepper together in a bowl. Stir in the milk and egg just until moistened. Stir in the parsley and green onions.

PER SERVING		DAILY GOAL	
Calories	465	2,000 (F), 2,500 (M)	
Total Fat	15 g	60 g or less (F), 70 g or less (M)	
Saturated fat	7 g	20 g or less (F), 23 g or less (M)	
Cholesterol	140 mg	300 mg or less	
Sodium	1,315 mg	2,400 mg or less	
Carbohydrates	47 g	250 g or more	
Protein	34 g	55 g to 90 g	

BUTTERMILK FRIED CHICKEN WITH PAN GRAVY

Don't rush to the skillet when preparing this extra-crispy, tender, and juicy fried chicken! The secret is allowing the coated chicken to chill briefly before frying. We promise the results are well worth the wait.

Prep time: 10 minutes plus chilling
Cooking time: 40 minutes
○ *Degree of difficulty: easy*

- 2 cups all-purpose flour
- 1 tablespoon salt
- 1 teaspoon freshly ground pepper
- 1½ cups low-fat buttermilk
- 2 chickens (3 pounds each), cut up
- 1 cup vegetable shortening
- ¼ cup butter *or* margarine

Pan Gravy
- 3 tablespoons flour
- 2 cups chicken broth
- 2 tablespoons milk

1 Combine the flour, salt, and pepper in a large bowl. Pour the buttermilk into another large bowl. Dip the chicken first in buttermilk, then in seasoned flour, shaking off any excess. Place chicken on a baking sheet lined with wax paper. Refrigerate, uncovered, for 1 hour.

2 Melt the shortening and butter in a heavy 12-inch skillet over medium heat to 375°F. Add half the chicken, skin side down; cover and cook for 10 minutes. Carefully turn pieces over, cover and cook until crisp and juices run clear when chicken is pierced, about 10 minutes more. Drain on paper towels. Keep warm.

3 Repeat with remaining chicken. Transfer to a serving platter. Keep warm.

Pan Gravy: Pour off all but 3 tablespoons of drippings from the skillet. Over medium heat whisk in the flour until smooth; cook 2 minutes. Add the chicken broth and milk, whisking until smooth. Simmer 2 minutes. Strain into a gravy boat. Serve with chicken. Makes 8 servings.

PER SERVING		DAILY GOAL
Calories	650	2,000 (F), 2,500 (M)
Total Fat	44 g	60 g or less (F), 70 g or less (M)
Saturated fat	14 g	20 g or less (F), 23 g or less (M)
Cholesterol	170 m	300 mg or less
Sodium	929 mg	2,400 mg or less
Carbohydrates	15 g	250 g or more
Protein	45 g	55 g to 90 g

CHICKEN À LA KING

Leftover chicken is never more elegant than when prepared in this classic rich cream sauce with mushrooms and pimiento.

Prep time: 10 minutes
Cooking time: 20 minutes
○ *Degree of difficulty: easy*

- 5 tablespoons butter *or* margarine, divided
- ½ pound fresh mushrooms, sliced
- 3 tablespoons flour
- 2 cups chicken broth
- ½ cup heavy *or* whipping cream
- 2 cups cubed cooked chicken
- 1 cup frozen peas, thawed
- ¼ cup chopped pimiento
- ¼ teaspoon freshly ground pepper
  Toast cups *or* toast points

1 Melt 2 tablespoons of the butter in a large skillet over medium heat. Add the mushrooms and cook for 5 minutes, stirring frequently. Remove mushrooms and set aside.

2 In the same skillet melt the remaining 3 tablespoons butter. Stir in the flour and blend until smooth. Cook 5 minutes.

3 Gradually add the chicken broth and cream, whisking constantly. Bring to a boil; cook for 5 minutes. Add mushrooms, chicken, peas and pimiento. Reduce heat and simmer for 5 minutes. Stir in the pepper. Spoon into toast cups or over toast points. Makes 4 servings.

PER SERVING		DAILY GOAL
Calories	445	2,000 (F), 2,500 (M)
Total Fat	32 g	60 g or less (F), 70 g or less (M)
Saturated fat	17 g	20 g or less (F), 23 g or less (M)
Cholesterol	14	2 mg 300 mg or less
Sodium	84	2 mg 2,400 mg or less
Carbohydrates	14g	250 g or more
Protein	25 g	55 g to 90 g

COUNTRY CAPTAIN

This American classic gained instant popularity at the former Hubert's restaurant in New York City. After we tried it in our Test Kitchen at Ladies' Home Journal, it became our all-time favorite too. As an extra bonus, the homemade curry spice mixture keeps indefinitely and is wonderful sautéed with vegetables, beef, or shrimp.

Prep time: 15 minutes
Cooking time: 65 to 70 minutes
● *Degree of difficulty: moderate*

1   **chicken (3 pounds), quartered**
¾   **teaspoon salt**
½   **teaspoon freshly ground pepper**
½   **cup all-purpose flour**
2   **tablespoons vegetable oil**
1   **medium onion, diced**
1   **teaspoon minced garlic**
1½ **tablespoons Curry Mixture (recipe at right)**
¼   **cup white wine *or* vermouth**
¾   **cup chicken broth**
1   **can (16 ounces) whole tomatoes, drained and chopped**
1   **red pepper, julienned**
1   **green pepper, julienned**
2   **tablespoons chutney**
2   **tablespoons currants *or* raisins**
1   **tablespoon butter *or* margarine**
3   **green onions, chopped**
    Toasted almond slivers, for garnish

1 Preheat oven to 375°F. Season the chicken with salt and pepper. Dredge in flour, shaking off any excess. In a large Dutch oven, heat the oil over medium-high heat. Add chicken skin side down and brown 10 minutes per side. Transfer chicken to a platter and keep warm.

2 Drain off all but 1 tablespoon of the drippings. Reduce heat to medium. Add the onion, garlic and Curry Mixture; sauté until onion is translucent, about 5 minutes. Add wine, scraping up any browned bits.

3 Add chicken broth, tomatoes, red and green peppers, chutney, and currants. Bring to a boil. Return chicken to Dutch oven. Cover; bake for 40 minutes.

4 Transfer chicken to a warm platter. Cook sauce over high heat; reduce until thick. Stir in butter and green onions. Add salt and pepper to taste. Pour over chicken and garnish with almonds. Serves 4.

PER SERVING		DAILY GOAL
Calories	605	2,000 (F), 2,500 (M)
Total Fat	31 g	60 g or less (F), 70 g or less (M)
Saturated fat	8 g	20 g or less (F), 23 g or less (M)
Cholesterol	139	300 mg or less
Sodium	991 mg	2,400 mg or less
Carbohydrates	35 g	250 g or more
Protein	46 g	55 g to 90 g

Curry Mixture
2   **tablespoons cumin**
2   **tablespoons coriander seed**
4   **bay leaves, crumbled**
1   **cinnamon stick, broken**
1   **tablespoon whole black peppercorns**
1   **teaspoon fennel seed**
1   **teaspoon tumeric**
½   **teaspoon allspice**

Grind all the ingredients in a blender to as fine a powder as possible. Shake through a sieve to remove seed hulls. (Store unused mixture in a jar with a tight-fitting lid.)

13

BRUNSWICK STEW

This southern stew was originally prepared with squirrel, but now chicken is a more popular choice. Both Virginia and Georgia claim this dish, which is chock full of okra, lima beans, tomatoes and corn.

Prep time: 30 minutes
Cooking time: 60 to 65 minutes
O *Degree of difficulty: easy*

- 1 **chicken (about 4 pounds), cut up**
- 1½ **teaspoons salt, divided**
- ½ **teaspoon freshly ground pepper**
- ¼ **teaspoon ground red pepper**
- ½ **cup all-purpose flour**
- 2 **tablespoons bacon fat *or* vegetable oil**
- 3 **cups sliced onions**
- 1 **teaspoon minced garlic**
- ½ **teaspoon rosemary, crushed**
- ½ **cup dry white wine**
- 1 **can (13¾ *or* 14½ ounces) chicken broth**
- 1 **can (14 ounces) whole tomatoes, chopped, liquid reserved**
- 1½ **pounds all-purpose potatoes, peeled and cut into ½-inch cubes**
- 1 **package (10 ounces) frozen whole-kernel corn**
- 1 **package (10 ounces) frozen baby lima beans**
- 8 **ounces okra, cut into 1-inch pieces, *or* 1 package (10 ounces) frozen okra**

1 Sprinkle the chicken with 1 teaspoon of the salt and both peppers, then coat with flour and shake off any excess. Heat the bacon fat or vegetable oil in a large skillet over medium-high heat. Add chicken to skillet and sauté, turning once, until browned, about 10 minutes. Transfer to a Dutch oven.

2 Add the onions, garlic, rosemary, and remaining ½ teaspoon salt to skillet; cook, stirring frequently, until onions are translucent, about 5 minutes. Pour in the wine and bring to a boil.

3 Add the wine mixture to the Dutch oven with the chicken broth and tomatoes and bring to a boil. Reduce heat, cover, and simmer for 30 minutes.

4 Stir in the potatoes, corn, lima beans, and okra. Simmer uncovered until tender, 30 to 35 minutes. Makes 8 servings.

PER SERVING		DAILY GOAL	
Calories	555	2,000 (F), 2,500 (M)	
Total Fat	27 g	60 g or less (F), 70 g or less (M)	
Saturated fat	8 g	20 g or less (F), 23 g or less (M)	
Cholesterol	118 mg	300 mg or less	
Sodium	900 mg	2,400 mg or less	
Carbohydrates	42 g	250 g or more	
Protein	37 g	55 g to 90 g	

NOTES

CLASSIC CHICKEN POTPIE

When it comes to the real thing, nothing beats this potpie. It takes some time and a bit of "T.L.C.," but its rich flavor and homey comfort are ample reward.

Prep time: 45 minutes plus cooling
Baking time: 1 hour 20 minutes
Degree of difficulty: moderate

- 1 **whole chicken (3 pounds)**
- 8 **cups water**
- 1 **onion, diced**
- 1 **carrot, diced**
- 1 **rib celery, diced**
- 1 **teaspoon thyme**
  Pastry for a double crust pie (not included)
- 1 **pint pearl onions**
- 2 **cups diced new potatoes**
- 1 **cup carrot chunks cut in ½-inch pieces**
- 2 **tablespoons butter** *or* **margarine**
- ⅓ **cup all-purpose flour**
- ½ **cup plus 1 tablespoon heavy** *or* **whipping cream, divided**
- 1 **teaspoon salt**
- ½ **teaspoon freshly ground pepper**
- 1 **cup frozen peas**
- 1 **cup frozen whole-kernel corn**
- ¼ **cup chopped fresh parsley**
- 1 **tablespoon fresh lemon juice**

1 Combine chicken with water, diced onion, carrot and celery, and thyme in a Dutch oven. Bring just to a boil. Reduce heat and simmer gently for 1 hour. Strain, reserving broth and chicken separately. Cool. Remove chicken from bones.

2 Skim fat from broth and reserve 3 cups.

3 Divide pastry in 6 pieces. Roll each piece between 2 sheets of wax paper to a 5-inch circle. Trim each pastry circle to fit the top of a 1½ cup ovenproof bowl; cut vents. For decorative design, reroll scraps and cut out. Refrigerate until ready to use.

4 Combine the pearl onions with water to cover in a saucepan. Bring to a boil; boil 5 minutes. Drain. When cool enough to handle, peel onions.

5 Combine the potatoes with 1 tablespoon of water in a 1-quart microwaveproof dish with lid; cover and microwave on high (100% power) 5 minutes. Remove with slotted spoon. Add the 1 cup of chunked carrots to dish and microwave on high (100% power) 2 minutes.

6 Preheat oven to 425°F. Melt butter in a large saucepan over medium heat. Whisk in the flour. Gradually whisk in the reserved 3 cups broth, ½ cup of the cream, salt, and pepper. Bring to boil, whisking occasionally.

7 Stir in chicken, pearl onions, potatoes, carrots, peas, and corn and return to a boil. Stir in the parsley and lemon juice and ladle into six ovenproof bowls. Top with pastry. Brush tops with remaining 1 tablespoon cream. Place on baking sheets and bake for 20 minutes. Makes 6 servings.

PER SERVING		DAILY GOAL
Calories	700	2,000 (F), 2,500 (M)
Total Fat	37 g	60 g or less (F), 70 g or less (M)
Saturated fat	14 g	20 g or less (F), 23 g or less (M)
Cholesterol	117 mg	300 mg or less
Sodium	943 mg	2,400 mg or less
Carbohydrates	60 g	250 g or more
Protein	33 g	55 g to 90 g

CHICKEN ROLLS WITH MUSHROOMS AND CREAM

Enjoy the rich, mellow flavor of roasted chicken in half the time it usually takes! These convenient chicken cutlets are rolled around herb stuffing, then quickly sautéed and served with creamy gravy.

Prep time: 25 minutes
Cooking time: 20 minutes
○ *Degree of difficulty: easy*

4 **tablespoons butter** *or* **margarine, divided**
1 **cup fresh bread crumbs**
2 **tablespoons chopped fresh parsley**
Pinch thyme
Salt
Freshly ground pepper
1½ **pounds chicken cutlets, about ½ inch thick**
½ **cup finely chopped shallots** *or* **onion**
2 **cups sliced fresh mushrooms**
½ **cup chicken broth**
½ **cup heavy** *or* **whipping cream**

1 Melt the butter in a large skillet over medium heat. Combine the bread crumbs, parsley, thyme, and a pinch each of salt and pepper in a bowl. Stir in 2 tablespoons of the melted butter until crumbs are moistened.

2 Sprinkle both sides of the chicken lightly with salt and pepper. Place 2 tablespoons of crumb mixture on the small end of each cutlet. Roll up each cutlet and secure with toothpicks.

3 Reheat remaining butter in the same skillet over medium-high heat. Add the chicken rolls and sauté until browned all over, about 5 minutes. Transfer to a plate.

4 Add the shallots to skillet and cook, stirring constantly, until translucent, about 1 minute. Add the mushrooms; cook until lightly browned, about 2 minutes more. Pour in the chicken broth and cream and bring to a boil.

5 Add chicken rolls, reduce heat, and simmer covered for 5 minutes. Turn rolls and simmer uncovered until chicken is cooked through and sauce is thickened, about 5 minutes more. Remove toothpicks from rolls. Makes 4 servings.

PER SERVING		DAILY GOAL
Calories	450	2,000 (F), 2,500 (M)
Total Fat	26 g	60 g or less (F), 70 g or less (M)
Saturated fat	15 g	20 g or less (F), 23 g or less (M)
Cholesterol	171 mg	300 mg or less
Sodium	477 mg	2,400 mg or less
Carbohydrates	12 g	250 g or more
Protein	43 g	55 g to 90 g

POULTRY HOTLINE

To answer any additional questions about chicken handling and safety, call the U.S. Department of Agriculture's Meat and Poultry Hotline. The toll-free number is (800) 535-4555. (In the Washington, D.C. area, call 447-3333.) The hotline hours are from 10 a.m. to 4 p.m. eastern time.

CHICKEN JAMBALAYA

Jambalaya is the signature chicken and rice dish of Cajun cooking. You'll love this version served with a spicy Creole Tomato Sauce.

Prep time: 20 minutes
Cooking time: 30 minutes
Degree of difficulty: easy

- ¾ **teaspoon salt**
- ½ **teaspoon thyme**
- ¼ **teaspoon onion powder**
- ¼ **teaspoon rubbed sage**
- ¼ **teaspoon freshly ground pepper**
- ¼ **teaspoon white pepper**
- **Pinch ground red pepper**
- 2 **tablespoons butter** *or* **margarine**
- ½ **pound smoked ham, diced (about 1½ cups)**
- ¾ **pound boneless, skinless chicken breast, diced**
- 1 **cup chopped onions**
- 1 **cup chopped celery**
- 1 **cup chopped green pepper**
- 1 **tablespoon minced garlic**
- 1½ **cups long-grain rice**
- 2½ **cups low-sodium chicken broth**
- 1 **cup chopped tomatoes**
- ½ **cup tomato sauce**

Creole Tomato Sauce
- ¼ **cup butter** *or* **margarine**
- 1 **cup chopped tomatoes**
- ¾ **cup finely chopped onion**
- ¾ **cup finely chopped celery**
- ¾ **cup finely chopped green pepper**
- ¾ **teaspoon salt**
- ¼ **teaspoon thyme**
- **Pinch onion powder**
- **Pinch freshly ground red and white peppercorns**
- 1½ **teaspoons minced garlic**
- 1¼ **cups low-sodium chicken broth**
- 1 **cup tomato sauce**
- 1 **teaspoon sugar**

1 In a cup combine the salt, thyme, onion powder, sage, and peppers.

2 Melt the butter in a Dutch oven over high heat. Add the ham and cook until browned, about 3 minutes. Add the chicken and 1 tablespoon of the spice mixture; brown 5 minutes, stirring.

3 Stir in the onions, celery, pepper, and garlic; cook until vegetables are tender, about 7 minutes. Stir in the rice, then the chicken broth, tomatoes, tomato sauce, and remaining spice mixture. Bring to a boil. Reduce heat, cover, and simmer about 20 minutes, stirring occasionally. Serve Jambalaya with sauce. Makes 6 servings.

Creole Tomato Sauce: Melt the butter in a skillet over high heat. Stir in the tomatoes, onion, celery, pepper, salt, thyme, onion powder, peppers, and garlic. Cook, stirring occasionally, until vegetables are tender, about 7 minutes. Stir in the chicken broth, tomato sauce, garlic, and sugar. Bring to a boil. Reduce heat and simmer uncovered 20 minutes. Makes 3 cups.

PER SERVING WITH 1/4 CUP SAUCE		DAILY GOAL
Calories	470	2,000 (F), 2,500 (M)
Total Fat	16 g	60 g or less (F), 70 g or less (M)
Saturated fat	8 g	20 g or less (F), 23 g or less (M)
Cholesterol	82 mg	300 mg or less
Sodium	1,687 mg	2,400 mg or less
Carbohydrates	55 g	250 g or more
Protein	28 g	55 g to 90 g

LOUISIANA CHICKEN AND SHRIMP GUMBO

This speedy version of the southern classic is perfect for one-pot entertaining. Serve in wide bowls with steamed rice.

▼ *Low-fat*
▽ *Low-calorie*
  Prep time: 5 minutes
  Cooking time: 30 minutes
○ *Degree of difficulty: easy*

  5 **slices (4 ounces) bacon**
 1½ **pounds skinless, boneless chicken thighs, halved**
  3 **tablespoons all-purpose flour**
  1 **cup chopped onions**
  1 **cup chopped celery**
  ½ **cup chopped green pepper**
  2 **teaspoons minced garlic**
  1 **can (13¾ or 14½ ounces) chicken broth**
  1 **bottle (8 ounces) clam juice**
  ½ **teaspoon salt**
  ¼ **teaspoon ground red pepper**
  ¼ **teaspoon white pepper**
  ¼ **teaspoon thyme**

  1 **pound medium shrimp, peeled and deveined**
  2 **tablespoons chopped fresh parsley**

1 Cook the bacon in a Dutch oven until crisp; drain on paper towels and crumble.

2 Discard all but 2 tablespoons of the drippings from Dutch oven. Brown the chicken in batches over high heat; transfer to a bowl.

3 Add the flour to Dutch oven; cook until browned. Add the onions, celery, green peppers, and garlic; cook about 5 minutes. Stir in the chicken broth, clam juice, salt, peppers, and thyme. Bring to a boil, stirring constantly. Reduce heat and simmer for 5 minutes.

4 Return chicken to Dutch oven; cook for 5 minutes more. Stir in the shrimp and cook about 2 minutes. Sprinkle with bacon and parsley. Makes 6 servings.

PER SERVING		DAILY GOAL
Calories	305	2,000 (F), 2,500 (M)
Total Fat	12 g	60 g or less (F), 70 g or less (M)
Saturated fat	3 g	20 g or less (F), 23 g or less (M)
Cholesterol	194 mg	300 mg or less
Sodium	923 mg	2,400 mg or less
Carbohydrates	8 g	250 g or more
Protein	38 g	55 g to 90 g

NOTES

_____
_____
_____
_____
_____
_____
_____
_____
_____
_____
_____
_____
_____
_____
_____
_____
_____
_____
_____
_____

ROAST CHICKEN WITH 20 CLOVES OF GARLIC

Don't flinch! Twenty cloves of garlic is correct, but this method of slow roasting brings out garlic's natural sweetness. When serving this tender chicken, plunge crusty French bread in the garlic-butter drippings—divine! *Also pictured on the cover.*

Prep time: 15 minutes
Cooking time: 1½ hours
Degree of difficulty: easy

1   **large head of garlic (about 20 cloves), separated and unpeeled**

2   **tablespoons butter *or* margarine, melted**

3½ **pounds chicken thighs *or* a 3½ pound broiler-fryer, cut up**

1½ **teaspoons salt**

½   **teaspoon freshly ground pepper
    Pinch nutmeg**

1 Preheat oven to 375°F. Trim ends off individual cloves of garlic and drop them into a pan of rapidly boiling water for about 10 seconds. Drain into a colander and run under cold water. Slip off the skins and set aside.

2 Place the melted butter in a small Dutch oven. Add the chicken to Dutch oven and toss to coat with butter. Lift out half the pieces.

3 Sprinkle pieces left in Dutch oven with half the garlic, salt, pepper, and nutmeg. Return remaining chicken to Dutch oven and repeat. Cover and bake for 1½ hours. (Do not open oven door during baking.) Serve with sliced French bread. Makes 6 servings.

PER SERVING		DAILY GOAL	
Calories	490	2,000 (F), 2,500 (M)	
Total Fat	35 g	60 g or less (F), 70 g or less (M)	
Saturated fat	12 g	20 g or less (F), 23 g or less (M)	
Cholesterol	186 mg	300 mg or less	
Sodium	749 mg	2,400 mg or less	
Carbohydrates	3 g	250 g or more	
Protein	37 g	55 g to 90 g	

21

ROASTED MINT CHICKEN

Chopped fresh mint and lemon are slipped under the skin of the chicken for maximum flavor without extra calories. Simply lift the skin away from the meat with your fingers or the handle of a wooden spoon and tuck the seasonings underneath.

Prep time: 10 minutes
Cooking time: 30 minutes
O *Degree of difficulty: easy*

½ cup chopped fresh mint, divided
2 teaspoons grated lemon peel
1 teaspoon minced garlic
1 chicken (3½ pounds), quartered
¼ teaspoon salt
⅛ teaspoon freshly ground pepper
3 tablespoons fresh lemon juice
1 tablespoon olive oil

1 Preheat oven to 450°F. Combine ¼ cup of the mint with the lemon peel and garlic in a cup. Spread the mixture under the skin of each chicken piece. Sprinkle chicken lightly with salt and pepper. Stir the remaining ¼ cup of mint with the lemon juice and oil in small bowl.

2 Arrange chicken skin side up in a shallow roasting pan. Brush with half the lemon juice mixture. Bake for 15 minutes. Brush with remaining lemon juice and bake about 15 minutes more, or until juices run clear when chicken is pierced with a fork. Makes 4 servings.

PER SERVING		DAILY GOAL
Calories	455	2,000 (F), 2,500 (M)
Total Fat	27 g	60 g or less (F), 70 g or less (M)
Saturated fat	7 g	20 g or less (F), 23 g or less (M)
Cholesterol	154 mg	300 mg or less
Sodium	279 mg	2,400 mg or less
Carbohydrates	2 g	250 g or more
Protein	48 g	55 g to 90 g

LET'S TOAST TO THE PERFECT ROAST

What's the secret to perfect roast chicken, with a crispy outside and a succulent inside? Start your bird in a hot 425°F. oven, then reduce the oven temperature to 375°F. to finish roasting. This will quickly cook the skin, forming a protective layer that seals the juicy meat underneath.

1 Preheat oven to 425°F. Remove the bag with neck, gizzards and any large visible pieces of fat from the main and neck cavity of a 3 to 3½ pound whole chicken. Rinse the chicken inside and out under cold water. Pat dry with paper towels. Place the chicken, breast side up, on a plastic cutting board or a work surface used only for chicken.

2 Stuff the cavity with 1 onion and ½ lemon, each cut into 4 wedges, and 2 or 3 sprigs of your favorite fresh herbs. (rosemary, thyme, sage, marjoram or combination). This steeps your chicken with flavor!

3 "Trussing" the chicken gives the bird a uniform shape during cooking and secures the stuffing. Tuck the wing tips under the wings by bending the fold under the back of the chicken. Cross the drumstick ends over the chicken cavity. Loop a cotton string around legs in a figure-eight pattern and tie securely.

4 We love roasting chicken on a bed of vegetables (which doubles as an oven rack!). This gives extra flavor to the chicken and makes wonderful pan juices.

ROAST HERB CHICKEN WITH BARLEY STUFFING

Here's the perfect Sunday supper for a crowd. The secret to the nutty flavor of the stuffing is sautèeing the barley until it is golden brown.

Prep time: 40 minutes
Cooking time: 2½ to 3 hours
Degree of difficulty: moderate

3 **tablespoons butter** *or* **margarine, divided**

1 **cup sliced fresh mushrooms**
1 **cup chopped onions**
1 **cup quick-cooking barley**
2½ **cups chicken broth** *or* **water**
½ **teaspoon salt**
¼ **teaspoon freshly ground pepper**
½ **cup chopped fresh parsley, divided**
1 **teaspoon minced fresh sage**
1 **whole roasting chicken (7 pounds)**
6 **to 10 sage leaves**

1 For the stuffing, melt 1 tablespoon of the butter in a medium saucepan over medium heat. Add the mushrooms and onions; sauté until translucent, about 5 minutes. Remove vegetables from pan; set aside.

Arrange 2 sliced carrots and 1 coarsely chopped onion in a roasting pan and place the chicken on top. To ensure crisp skin and an even golden color, brush chicken lightly with 1 teaspoon olive oil. Sprinkle with salt and freshly ground pepper.

5 Place in the hot oven and roast for 15 minutes. Reduce the heat to 375°F. and continue roasting for 45 minutes or until the juices run clear, not pink, when thickest part of one thigh is pierced with a long fork. Or, insert a meat thermometer

in the thickest part of the thigh without touching the bone. The temperature should register 180°F. when the chicken is done.

6 Cover the chicken loosely with foil and let it stand for 15 minutes. Carefully transfer the chicken to a warm serving platter. Skim the fat from the pan juices, season to taste, and serve with the cooked vegetables.

2 Melt the remaining 2 tablespoons butter in pan. Add the barley and cook until golden brown, about 3 minutes. Add the chicken broth, salt, and pepper. Bring to a boil. Simmer uncovered until barley is tender and liquid is absorbed, about 20 minutes. Stir in the onion mixture, ⅓ cup of the parsley and the minced sage. Cool completely before stuffing chicken.

3 Preheat oven to 350°F. Rinse the chicken and pat it dry. Remove giblets and excess fat from body cavity; discard. Rub additional salt and pepper over chicken. Stuff cavity with barley mixture; close with skewers.

4 Lift skin from the breast. Tuck the remaining parsley and the whole sage leaves under skin.

5 Tie the legs together with string and tuck wings under. Place on a rack in a roasting pan. Roast for 2½ to 3 hours, until a meat thermometer inserted in thickest part of the thigh reaches 180°F. Transfer chicken to a serving platter and let stand 15 minutes before carving. Makes 8 servings.

PER SERVING		DAILY GOAL
Calories	580	2,000 (F), 2,500 (M)
Total Fat	32 g	60 g or less (F), 70 g or less (M)
Saturated fat	10 g	20 g or less (F), 23 g or less (M)
Cholesterol	167 mg	300 mg or less
Sodium	558 mg	2,400 mg or less
Carbohydrates	16 g	250 g or more
Protein	52 g	55 g to 90 g

SUNDAY'S ROASTED CHICKEN WITH BULGUR STUFFING

This oven-baked feast is a nutritional bonanza: The subtly sweet stuffing abounds with fiber, the sweet potatoes with beta carotene, and the broccoli with vitamin C.

▼ *Low-fat*
Prep time: 35 minutes plus standing
Cooking time: 2 to 2½ hours
○ *Degree of difficulty: easy*

1	whole roasting chicken (6 to 7 pounds)
	Salt
	Freshly ground pepper
6	pounds sweet potatoes, scrubbed
½	cup white wine
½	cup chicken broth
1½	pounds broccoli, trimmed, cut into large florets, and steamed just before serving

Bulgur Stuffing

2	teaspoons vegetable oil
1	cup minced onions
⅔	cup bulgur wheat
1	cup chicken broth
¼	cup diced dried apricots
¼	cup raisins
¼	cup chopped fresh flat leaf parsley
1	teaspoon grated orange peel
½	teaspoon freshly ground pepper

1 One hour before roasting, remove the chicken from refrigerator. Preheat oven to 350°F. Remove the giblets and excess fat from body cavity and discard. Rinse chicken and pat dry. Fill the cavity with stuffing and tie legs together with string. Tuck wings under. Sprinkle chicken with salt and pepper.

2 Place the chicken in a roasting pan and roast for 2 to 2½ hours, until a meat thermometer inserted in the thickest part of the thigh registers 180°F.

3 Meanwhile, arrange the sweet potatoes in a baking dish. After chicken has roasted 30 minutes, put sweet potatoes in oven and roast about 1½ hours or until very tender.

4 Transfer chicken to a serving platter and let stand 15 minutes before carving.

5 Pour the wine and broth over drippings in roasting pan. Bring to a boil over medium-high heat, stirring to break up browned bits; boil 2 minutes. Skim fat. Makes 1⅓ cups.

6 Serve chicken with sauce, sweet potatoes and broccoli. Makes 6 servings.

Bulgur Stuffing: Heat the oil in a medium saucepan over medium-low heat. Add the onions, cover and cook, stirring occasionally, until tender, about 5 minutes. Stir in the bulgur and cook for 1 minute. Stir in the chicken broth, apricots, and raisins. Bring to a boil. Reduce heat to low; cover and cook until broth is absorbed, about 10 minutes. Stir in parsley, orange peel, and pepper. Cool completely before stuffing chicken. Makes 2¾ cups.

PER SERVING WITH 3 OUNCES OF CHICKEN		DAILY GOAL
Calories	675	2,000 (F), 2,500 (M)
Total Fat	12 g	60 g or less (F), 70 g or less (M)
Saturated fat	2 g	20 g or less (F), 23 g or less (M)
Cholesterol	76 mg	300 mg or less
Sodium	431 mg	2,400 mg or less
Carbohydrates	106 g	250 g or more
Protein	35 g	55 g to 90 g

CHICKEN SPANS

THE GLOBE

Come and discover the world-wide tastes of chicken. Revered in cuisines all across the globe, you'll find chicken stewing in the French classic Coq au Vin and Italy's Chicken Cacciatore. You'll love stir-frying tender nuggets of chicken with fresh crisp vegetables in a delicious Thai dish, or baking chicken to golden perfection in the Tandoori-style from India. Whatever country's cuisine you choose, chicken's versatility is deliciously evident.

TANDOORI CHICKEN

In this classic Indian dish, chicken is marinated in seasoned yogurt and cooked in a special clay oven for an incredibly tender and flavorful bird. By grilling over low heat, you can achieve the same delicious results.

▽ *Low-calorie*
   Prep time: 15 minutes plus chilling
      and standing
   Cooking time: 30 minutes
○ *Degree of difficulty: easy*

1 **teaspoon cumin**
½ **teaspoon coriander**
1 **teaspoon paprika**
½ **teaspoon ground red pepper**
1 **container (8 ounces) plain yogurt**
3 **tablespoons fresh lemon juice**
1 **tablespoon minced fresh ginger**
1 **teaspoon minced garlic**
1 **teaspoon salt**
1 **chicken (3 to 3½ pounds), cut up**
   Lemon wedges

1 Heat the cumin, coriander, paprika, and red pepper in small saucepan over medium-low heat, stirring until fragrant, 1 to 2 minutes. (Be careful not to burn.) Transfer spice mixture to a large glass bowl and stir in the yogurt, lemon juice, ginger, garlic, and salt.

2 Remove skin from the chicken, except wings, and score flesh diagonally ½-inch deep with a small sharp knife. Toss chicken with yogurt mixture. Cover and refrigerate overnight.

3 Remove chicken from refrigerator 1 hour before cooking. To grill: Prepare the grill for indirect heat. Place disposable foil roasting pan in bottom center of grill. Arrange 20 charcoal briquettes on 2 opposite sides of foil pan. Ignite charcoal. When white ash has formed, grill chicken over low coals about 30 minutes, turning every 10 minutes, until the juices run clear when when the chicken is pierced with a fork. Serve with lemon wedges. Makes 4 servings.

To broil: Preheat the broiler and broiler pan. Broil chicken 5 inches from heat source for 30 minutes, turning as directed for grilling.

PER SERVING		DAILY GOAL
Calories	285	2,000 (F), 2,500 (M)
Total Fat	11 g	60 g or less (F), 70 g or less (M)
Saturated fat	3 g	20 g or less (F), 23 g or less (M)
Cholesterol	119 mg	300 mg or less
Sodium	408 mg	2,400 mg or less
Carbohydrates	3 g	250 g or more
Protein	40 g	55 g to 90 g

NOTES

JAMAICAN JERK CHICKEN

This spicy Jamaican specialty, served in "jerk shacks" all over the island, has been popular since the days of Columbus. Here, the traditional flavors of ginger, pepper, and allspice simmer until the chicken is tender enough to be "jerked" from the bone.

▽ *Low-calorie*
   Prep time: 10 minutes plus marinating
   Cooking time: 40 minutes
◯ *Degree of difficulty: easy*

6 **whole chicken legs**
2 **teaspoons ginger**
1 **teaspoon paprika**
½ **teaspoon ground red pepper**
½ **teaspoon allspice**
½ **teaspoon salt**
¼ **teaspoon freshly ground pepper**
2 **tablespoons vegetable oil**
3½ **cups chopped onions**
1 **tablespoon minced garlic**
¾ **cup chicken broth**
1 **can (8 ounces) tomato sauce**

1 Remove skin from the chicken. Combine the ginger, paprika, red pepper, allspice, salt, and pepper in large bowl. Add chicken and toss to coat. Cover and refrigerate for 1 to 24 hours.

2 Heat the oil in a large skillet over medium-high heat. Add chicken and cook until browned, about 4 minutes per side. Transfer to a plate.

3 Discard all but 1 tablespoon of drippings from skillet. Add the onions and cook covered until translucent, about 4 minutes. Stir in the garlic and cook 30 seconds. Carefully add the chicken broth and tomato sauce.

4 Return chicken to skillet. Bring to a boil. Reduce heat and simmer covered for 30 minutes. Transfer chicken to a platter. Season sauce to taste with salt and pepper and pour over chicken. Makes 6 servings.

PER SERVING		DAILY GOAL
Calories	245	2,000 (F), 2,500 (M)
Total Fat	9 g	60 g or less (F), 70 g or less (M)
Saturated fat	2 g	20 g or less (F), 23 g or less (M)
Cholesterol	104 mg	300 mg or less
Sodium	671 mg	2,400 mg or less
Carbohydrates	12 g	250 g or more
Protein	28 g	55 g to 90 g

CHICKEN SATAY WITH SPICY PEANUT SAUCE

This specialty from Indonesia is most often enjoyed as an appetizer or snack. Served with tossed greens or a cucumber salad, these tasty morsels of chicken also make a wonderful light entrée. *Also pictured on page 26.*

▽ *Low-calorie*
Prep time: 20 minutes plus marinating
Cooking time: 6 to 8 minutes
○ *Degree of difficulty: easy*

 2 teaspoons curry powder
 1 teaspoon grated fresh ginger
 1 teaspoon minced garlic
 ½ cup unsweetened coconut milk
 1 tablespoon minced fresh
   lemongrass *or* 1 teaspoon grated
   lemon peel
 ½ teaspoon red pepper flakes
 ½ teaspoon salt
 1 pound boneless, skinless chicken
   breasts, cut into ½-inch strips

Spicy Peanut Sauce
 ½ teaspoon ground coriander
 ½ teaspoon grated fresh ginger
 ½ teaspoon minced garlic
 ¼ teaspoon red pepper flakes
 ½ cup plus 2 tablespoons
   unsweetened coconut milk
 1½ teaspoons creamy peanut butter
 1 teaspoon fresh lime juice
 ½ teaspoon Oriental fish sauce
   (nuoc mam) *or* soy sauce

1 Soak 8 wooden skewers in water for at least 30 minutes.

2 Meanwhile, heat a small skillet over medium-high heat. Add the curry powder, ginger, and garlic; cook, stirring, until curry is fragrant and slightly browned, about 1 minute.

3 Transfer to a bowl and add the coconut milk, lemongrass, red pepper flakes, and salt. Add the chicken and stir to coat. Marinate at room temperature for 30 minutes. Preheat broiler or grill for direct heat.

4 Weave chicken loosely onto skewers. Grill or broil 3 inches from heat source for 3 to 4 minutes per side or until firm. Serve with Spicy Peanut Sauce. Makes 4 servings.

Spicy Peanut Sauce: Heat a small skillet over medium-high heat. Add the coriander, ginger, garlic, and red pepper flakes. Cook, stirring, until fragrant and coriander begins to brown, about 30 seconds to 1 minute. Combine coconut milk, peanut butter, lime juice, and fish sauce in a small bowl. Add heated spice mixture; whisk until smooth. Makes about 1 cup.

PER SERVING WITH 1/4 CUP SAUCE		DAILY GOAL
Calories	240	2,000 (F), 2,500 (M)
Total Fat	13 g	60 g or less (F), 70 g or less (M)
Saturated fat	10 g	20 g or less (F), 23 g or less (M)
Cholesterol	66 mg	300 mg or less
Sodium	225 mg	2,400 mg or less
Carbohydrates	3 g	250 g or more
Protein	28 g	55 g to 90 g

NOTES

_____

_____

_____

_____

_____

_____

HOT 'N' HEALTHY CHICKEN: HANDLE THIS BIRD WITH CARE

There is a growing number of chicken choices available at the supermarket to suit everyone's taste and budget. Shoppers can choose among whole, cut up, boneless, skinless, ground, and dark or light meat varieties. But, when it comes to safely selecting, storing, and thawing chicken, just a few simple rules apply.

1 When purchasing chicken, always check the "Sell By" date on the package label. Look for unblemished skin, with no obvious bruises. Depending on the chicken's diet, the skin color will range from white to deep yellow. This does not reflect any difference in flavor, tenderness or nutritional value. What's most important is that the meat has a fresh, clean aroma.

2 Refrigerate raw chicken immediately; never leave it on the countertop at room temperature. If you are storing packaged fresh chicken in its original wrapping, place it in the coldest part of the refrigerator (usually the meat tray). Fresh, raw, whole chicken, chicken parts, and ground chicken can be refrigerated at 40°F. for up to 2 days; afterwards it must be frozen.

3 Cooked, cut up chicken can be refrigerated up to 2 days. If a chicken is stuffed, transfer the stuffing to a separate container before chilling.

4 When wrapping chicken for the freezer, first rinse the chicken and pat it dry with paper towels. Be sure the packaging is airtight. We recommend a double thickness of plastic wrap, heavy-duty plastic freezer bags, or containers with airtight seals. Frozen and properly wrapped, chicken can be frozen at 0°F. for 4 to 6 months.

5 Cooked chicken may be frozen using the method for uncooked chicken. Cooked chicken can be frozen at 0° F. for 2 to 3 months. For cooked chicken prepared in a sauce or gravy, use a rigid freezer-proof container with a tight-fitting lid.

6 Frozen uncooked chicken may be thawed in the refrigerator, in cold water or in the microwave. (Never thaw chicken on the countertop at room temperature.) Thawed in the refrigerator, a 4-pound whole chicken takes about 24 hours and cut up parts take 3 to 9 hours. To thaw safely in cold water, completely immerse the chicken in its original wrapping or a water-tight plastic bag, changing the water often. It will take about 2 hours to thaw a whole chicken. Thawing times in the microwave will vary according to the size of the chicken pieces. Arrange the chicken on a microwave-proof plate. Microwave on defrost (10% power) or medium-low (30% power) for 2 minutes. Let stand 2 minutes. Repeat if needed, turning and separating chicken pieces as they thaw. (Take care that the chicken does not begin to cook.)

7 Once properly thawed, chicken should not be refrozen. This lowers the quality of its flavor and texture.

CHICKEN WITH CAPER CREAM

Inspired by the warm and sunny flavors of the Mediterranean, this no-fuss entrée is perfect for family or friends. You can easily substitute a whole chicken, cut up, for the bone-in breasts.

▽ *Low-calorie*
Prep time: 20 minutes
Cooking time: 25 minutes
○ *Degree of difficulty: easy*

2 **tablespoons butter** *or* **margarine**
4 **chicken breast halves (2½ pounds)**
2 **tablespoons white wine vinegar**
¾ **cup heavy** *or* **whipping cream**
1 **tablespoon capers, drained**
½ **bay leaf**
½ **teaspoon oregano, crushed**
¼ **teaspoon freshly ground pepper**

1 Preheat oven to 350°F. Melt the butter in a large skillet over medium heat. Add the chicken; cook until browned, about 4 minutes per side. Transfer to a 12x7-inch ovenproof dish.

2 Pour off the drippings from skillet. Add the vinegar to skillet; cook 30 seconds. Stir in the cream, capers, bay leaf, oregano, and pepper. Bring to a boil, stirring up any browned bits; boil 2 minutes.

3 Pour the sauce over chicken. Bake uncovered for 25 minutes. Discard bay leaf. Makes 4 servings.

PER SERVING		DAILY GOAL
Calories	320	2,000 (F), 2,500 (M)
Total Fat	22 g	60 g or less (F), 70 g or less (M)
Saturated fat	13 g	20 g or less (F), 23 g or less (M)
Cholesterol	139 mg	300 mg or less
Sodium	190 mg	2,400 mg or less
Carbohydrates	2 g	250 g or more
Protein	27 g	55 g to 90 g

CHICKEN PAPRIKASH

Paprika is a spice made by grinding sweet red pepper pods to a fine powder. Its flavor can range from mild and sweet to hot and complex. The finest variety is considered to be from Hungary, hence the origin of this classic chicken dish.

Prep time: 10 minutes
Cooking time: 50 minutes
○ *Degree of difficulty: easy*

1 **small chicken (2½ pounds), cut up**
2½ **teaspoons Hungarian** *or* **regular paprika, divided**
1 **tablespoon vegetable oil**
1 **large onion, chopped**
¾ **cup chicken broth**
1 **teaspoon salt**
¾ **cup sour cream**

1 Combine the chicken and 1 teaspoon of the paprika in a large bowl, tossing to coat. Heat the oil in a large skillet over medium-high heat. Cook chicken until browned on all sides, about 5 minutes. Remove from skillet and set aside.

2 Add the onion to the skillet and cook until translucent, about 3 minutes. Return chicken to skillet. Add the chicken broth and salt; bring to a boil. Reduce heat, cover, and simmer until chicken is tender, about 40 minutes. Transfer chicken with a slotted spoon to a warm serving platter.

3 Stir the remaining 1½ teaspoons paprika and sour cream into the drippings in skillet and heat just until hot, being careful not to boil. Immediately spoon sauce over chicken. Makes 4 servings.

PER SERVING		DAILY GOAL
Calories	570	2,000 (F), 2,500 (M)
Total Fat	42 g	60 g or less (F), 70 g or less (M)
Saturated fat	14 g	20 g or less (F), 23 g or less (M)
Cholesterol	164	300 mg or less
Sodium	928 mg	2,400 mg or less
Carbohydrates	8 g	250 g or more
Protein	38 g	55 g to 90 g

CHICKEN COUSCOUS

This regal dish from the Middle East is easy on your pocketbook and perfect for casual entertaining.

▼   *Low-fat*
     Prep time: 10 minutes
     Cooking time: 35 minutes
◯   *Degree of difficulty: easy*

2   **teaspoons olive oil**
1   **pound boneless, skinless chicken thighs, cut into 1½ -inch pieces**
     Salt
     Freshly ground pepper
¼   **teaspoon turmeric**
     Pinch saffron powder
1   **cup chopped onions**
2   **cans (13¾ or 14½ ounces each) chicken broth, divided**
1   **can (14 ounces) plum tomatoes, drained**
½   **pound turnips, peeled and cubed**
10 **pearl onions (3 ounces), peeled**
1   **cinnamon stick (3 inches)**
2   **sprigs fresh parsley**
2   **sprigs plus 2 tablespoons chopped fresh cilantro**

2   **small zucchini (½ pound), sliced ¼-inch thick**
½   **cup frozen baby peas**
1   **jalapeño chili, minced *or* ¼ teaspoon red pepper flakes**
1   **cup quick-cooking couscous (semolina)**

1 Heat the oil in a large skillet over medium-high heat. Pat the chicken dry and season it with salt and pepper. Add to skillet with the turmeric and saffron. Cook until browned, about 3 minutes per side. Stir in the chopped onions and cook for 2 minutes more.

2 Add 1 can of the chicken broth and the tomatoes (breaking them up with a spoon), turnips, pearl onions, cinnamon stick, parsley, and cilantro sprigs; cook until liquid is reduced by three quarters, 20 minutes. Add the zucchini, peas and jalapeño chili. Bring to a simmer and cook for 2 minutes.

3 Meanwhile, make couscous according to package directions with the remaining can of chicken broth instead of water. Stir in the chopped cilantro. Spoon couscous on a platter and top with chicken mixture. Makes 4 servings.

PER SERVING		DAILY GOAL
Calories	442	2,000 (F), 2,500 (M)
Total Fat	10 g	60 g or less (F), 70 g or less (M)
Saturated fat	2 g	20 g or less (F), 23 g or less (M)
Cholesterol	99 mg	300 mg or less
Sodium	1,473 mg	2,400 mg or less
Carbohydrates	54 g	250 g or more
Protein	32 g	55 g to 90 g

NOTES

MADRAS CHICKEN CURRY IN SPICY PUFFS

This unusual entrée is perfect party food that can be completely prepared ahead. Have your guests fill their own puffs, adding the condiments of their choice.

▽ *Low-calorie*
Prep time: 30 minutes
Cooking time: 15 minutes
○ *Degree of difficulty: easy*

1 tablespoon vegetable oil
1 cup finely chopped onions
½ cup finely chopped red pepper
½ cup finely chopped carrots
1 tablespoon hot curry powder
½ teaspoon cumin
½ teaspoon coriander
4½ cups cooked chicken (about 1 pound, boneless), shredded and minced
¾ cup heavy *or* whipping cream
¾ cup chicken broth
½ teaspoon salt
½ teaspoon freshly ground pepper
1 green onion, chopped

2 tablespoons unsweetened shredded coconut
Condiments: prepared chutney, chopped salted peanuts, and shredded coconut
Spicy Puffs (recipe at right)

1 Heat the oil in a large skillet over medium heat. Add the onions, red pepper, carrots, curry powder, cumin, and coriander. Cover and cook, stirring occasionally, until vegetables are tender, about 8 minutes.

2 Increase heat to medium-high. Add the chicken, cream, and chicken broth; cook until sauce is thickened, about 5 minutes. Season with salt and pepper. (Can be made ahead. Cover and refrigerate up to 24 hours. Reheat in skillet, stirring, over medium heat.) Transfer to a serving dish and top with the green onion and coconut. Serve with condiments and Spicy Puffs. Makes 4½ cups.

PER SERVING		DAILY GOAL
Calories	25	2,000 (F), 2,500 (M)
Total Fat	2 g	60 g or less (F), 70 g or less (M)
Saturated fat	.8 g	20 g or less (F), 23 g or less (M)
Cholesterol	9 mg	300 mg or less
Sodium	34 mg	2,400 mg or less
Carbohydrates	0 g	250 g or more
Protein	2 g	55 g to 90 g

SPICY PUFFS

▽ *Low-calorie*
Prep time: 40 minutes
Cooking time: 25 minutes
○ *Degree of difficulty: easy*

1 cup water
½ cup butter *or* margarine
1 tablespoon sugar
1 teaspoon cumin
½ teaspoon coriander
½ teaspoon salt
½ teaspoon freshly ground pepper
⅛ teaspoon ground red pepper
1 cup all-purpose flour
4 large eggs, at room temperature

1 Preheat oven to 400°F. Grease 2 cookie sheets. Heat the water, butter or margarine, sugar, cumin, coriander, salt, pepper, and ground red pepper in a large saucepan.

2 Add the flour all at once, stirring vigorously, until batter leaves sides of pan. Cool 2 minutes. Add the eggs, at room temperature, one at a time, beating well after each addition, until batter is smooth.

3 Place the batter in a pastry bag with ½-inch plain tip. Pipe 1½-inch puffs on prepared cookie sheets. Bake 25 minutes or until firm to the touch and golden brown.

4 When the puffs are cool enough to handle, cut off the tops and remove wet dough inside. (Can be made ahead. Freeze up to one month. When ready to serve, reheat in preheated 400°F. oven 10 minutes or until hot and crisp.) Makes 5 dozen.

PER PUFF		DAILY GOAL
Calories	30	2,000 (F), 2,500 (M)
Total Fat	2 g	60 g or less (F), 70 g or less (M)
Saturated fat	1 g	20 g or less (F), 23 g or less (M)
Cholesterol	19 mg	300 mg or less
Sodium	39 mg	2,400 mg or less
Carbohydrates	2 g	250 g or more
Protein	1 g	55 g to 90 gow

HOW MUCH TO BUY?

When purchasing a whole chicken, broiler-fryer or roaster, figure ½ pound per serving.

BRAZILIAN CHICKEN WITH FRUIT

Chicken paired with fruit is widely popular in Latin America and in this dish, coconut milk adds a special creaminess. Look for the unsweetened product in the Oriental foods section of your supermarket.

Prep time: 20 minutes
Cooking time: 20 minutes
○ *Degree of difficulty: easy*

1 **tablespoon flour**
¾ **teaspoon salt, divided**
¼ **teaspoon freshly ground pepper**
2 **pounds chicken thighs, skinned**
1 **tablespoon vegetable oil**
½ **cup chopped onion**
1 **teaspoon minced garlic**
½ **cup unsweetened coconut milk**
½ **cup chicken broth**
½ **cup (4 ounces) whole pitted dates**
2 **tablespoons fresh lime juice**
1 **teaspoon grated lime peel**
1 **teaspoon grated orange peel**
¼ **teaspoon ground red pepper**
½ **fresh pineapple, peeled and sliced**
1 **small papaya, peeled and sliced**
   Lime wedges, for garnish

1 Place flour, ¼ teaspoon of the salt, and the pepper in a small bowl. Pat the chicken dry and sprinkle with flour mixture. Heat the oil in a large skillet over medium-high heat. Add chicken and cook until browned, about 3 minutes per side. Add the onion and garlic; cook until translucent, about 2 minutes.

2 Add the coconut milk, chicken broth, dates, lime juice, lime peel, orange peel, remaining ½ teaspoon salt, and ground red pepper to the skillet. Reduce heat to medium and cook, covered for 10 minutes, stirring occasionally. Serve with pineapple and papaya slices. Garnish with lime wedges. Makes 4 servings.

PER SERVING		DAILY GOAL
Calories	405	2,000 (F), 2,500 (M)
Total Fat	15 g	60 g or less (F), 70 g or less (M)
Saturated fat	7 g	20 g or less (F), 23 g or less (M)
Cholesterol	107 mg	300 mg or less
Sodium	676 mg	2,400 mg or less
Carbohydrates	43 g	250 g or more
Protein	28 g	55 g to 90 g

37

THAI CHICKEN WITH VEGETABLES

This southeast Asian stir-fry makes the most of three ingredients: chilies for heat, lemon grass for citrus flavor, and mint or basil for fresh taste.

▼ *Low-fat*
Prep time: 35 minutes
Cooking time: 13 minutes
○ *Degree of difficulty: easy*

3 teaspoons vegetable oil, divided
1 tablespoon minced lemon grass *or*
   1 teaspoon grated lemon peel
2 teaspoons minced garlic
2 teaspoons minced fresh ginger
4 fresh Thai red *or* green chilies,
   seeded and sliced thin, *or*
   1 teaspoon red pepper flakes
1 pound boneless, skinless chicken
   breast, sliced into ½-inch strips
2 cups green onions, cut into
   2-inch pieces
½ teaspoon salt
½ pound green beans, halved
2 cups julienned carrots
1 cup chicken broth
½ cup chopped fresh mint *or* fresh
   basil leaves
3 cups hot cooked rice

1 Heat 2 teaspoons of the oil over high heat in a large non-stick skillet. Add the lemon grass or lemon peel, garlic, ginger, and chilies; cook for 15 seconds. Add the chicken and green onions; sprinkle with salt. Cook, stirring, until golden about 3 to 5 minutes. Transfer to a plate.

2 Add the remaining 1 teaspoon oil to skillet. Add the beans and carrots; cook, stirring, for 1 minute. Add the chicken broth; cook until vegetables are tender, about 3 to 5 minutes more. Return chicken mixture to skillet; heat through. Transfer to a serving dish and sprinkle with mint. Serve with rice. Makes 4 servings.

PER SERVING		DAILY GOAL	
Calories	420	2,000 (F), 2,500 (M)	
Total Fat	6 g	60 g or less (F), 70 g or less (M)	
Saturated fat	1 g	20 g or less (F), 23 g or less (M)	
Cholesterol	66 mg	300 mg or less	
Sodium	599 mg	2,400 mg or less	
Carbohydrates	57 g	250 g or more	
Protein	33 g	55 g to 90 g	

39

JAPANESE CHICKEN WINGS

Slightly sweetened with sake wine and fresh ginger, these tasty appetizers can be enjoyed either hot or at room temperature.

▽ *Low-calorie*
   Prep time: 15 to 20 minutes
   Cooking time: 20 minutes
○ *Degree of difficulty: easy*

2   **pounds chicken wings, tips trimmed**
½   **cup soy sauce**
½   **cup sake**
¼   **cup sugar**
¼   **teaspoon red pepper flakes**
1   **garlic clove, crushed**
1½ **teaspoon grated fresh ginger**

1   Preheat oven to 375°F. Cut each wing into 2 pieces at joint.

2   Combine the soy sauce, sake, sugar, red pepper flakes, garlic, and ginger in a 13x9-inch baking dish. Add wing pieces and turn to coat well. Let marinate at room temperature for 1 hour. (Can be made ahead. Cover and refrigerate up to 24 hours.)

3   Bake chicken uncovered in marinade for 1½ hours, turning occasionally. Makes 4 servings.

PER SERVING		DAILY GOAL
Calories	195	2,000 (F), 2,500 (M)
Total Fat	17 g	60 g or less (F), 70 g or less (M)
Saturated fat	3.5 g	20 g or less (F), 23 g or less (M)
Cholesterol	72 mg	300 mg or less
Sodium	2,013 mg	2,400 mg or less
Carbohydrates	10 g	250 g or more
Protein	24 g	55 g to 90 g

THE SIMPLEST CHICKEN BROTH: IT'S ALL IN THE CAN.

In a pinch, canned chicken broth is an excellent substitution for homemade stock. Here are a few guidelines to keep in mind:

1   When using condensed chicken broth for homemade stock, dilute the broth with an equal amount of water.

2   Low-sodium chicken broth and regular chicken broth can be used interchangeably.

3   If you wish to reduce canned broth for a stronger flavor in a sauce, use the low-sodium variety.

4   To enrich the flavor of canned broth, combine the desired amount of broth in a saucepan with a few sprigs fresh parsley, a couple of crushed garlic cloves and a pinch of thyme. Simmer 15 minutes, strain, then proceed with the recipe as directed.

5   To skim the fat from canned chicken broth, place it in the freezer for 30 minutes or refrigerate it 4 hours or overnight. Spoon off fat.

NOTES

_____

_____

_____

_____

_____

_____

_____

FIVE-SPICE CHICKEN

Chinese five-spice powder is a blend of cinnamon, cloves, star anise, fennel and pepper, and is widely available. This chicken is skinless to save calories, but it's cooked with the bone for maximum flavor.

Ⓜ *Microwave*
▼ *Low-fat*
▽ *Low-calorie*
　 Prep time: 10 minutes
　 Microwave time: 12 minutes
○ *Degree of difficulty: easy*

1 **tablespoon brown sugar**
3 **tablespoons dry sherry**
2 **tablespoons soy sauce**
1 **teaspoon minced fresh ginger**
1 **teaspoon minced garlic**
¼ **teaspoon Chinese five-spice powder**
4 **chicken thighs (1½ pounds), skinned**
1 **teaspoon cornstarch**
1 **tablespoon cold water**
2 **green onions, sliced thin, for garnish**

1 In a shallow 1½ -quart microwave-proof dish combine the brown sugar, sherry, soy sauce, ginger, garlic, and five-spice powder. Add the chicken and turn to coat. Cover and microwave on high (100% power) for 10 minutes, turning chicken halfway through. Transfer chicken to a platter; keep warm.

2 Dissolve the cornstarch in cold water and stir into pan juices. Microwave uncovered on high (100% power) for 1½ minutes more. Stir the sauce and pour over chicken. Garnish with the green onions. Makes 4 servings.

PER SERVING		DAILY GOAL
Calories	145	2,000 (F), 2,500 (M)
Total Fat	4 g	60 g or less (F), 70 g or less (M)
Saturated fat	1 g	20 g or less (F), 23 g or less (M)
Cholesterol	81 mg	300 mg or less
Sodium	601 mg	2,400 mg or less
Carbohydrates	6 g	250 g or more
Protein	20 g	55 g to 90 g

CHINESE HACKED CHICKEN

Chicken is considered a noble bird in Chinese culture and is served on special occasions. In this dish it is tossed with fragrant sesame flavored noodles.

Prep time: 30 minutes plus standing
Cooking time: 10 minutes
○ *Degree of difficulty: easy*

4   boneless, skinless chicken breast
    halves (about 1 pound)
1   teaspoon salt
¼   cup tahini (sesame paste)
3   tablespoons soy sauce, divided
2   teaspoons distilled white vinegar
2   teaspoons minced fresh ginger
1   teaspoon sugar
1   teaspoon minced garlic
1   teaspoon Oriental sesame oil,
    divided
¼   teaspoon red pepper sauce
1   tablespoon vegetable oil
1   package (9 ounces) fresh *or* dried
    angel hair pasta (cappellini)

1   cucumber, peeled, seeded, and
    julienned
1   red pepper, julienned
3   green onions, julienned
1   tablespoon toasted sesame seed

1 Combine the chicken breasts with the salt and enough water to cover in medium saucepan. Bring just to a boil. Reduce heat. Cover and simmer gently for 10 minutes; cool to room temperature.

2 Remove chicken, reserving poaching liquid. Cut chicken into strips.

3 Combine the tahini, 1 tablespoon of the soy sauce, vinegar, ginger, sugar, garlic, ½ teaspoon of the sesame oil, and the red pepper sauce in a medium bowl. Whisk in ¼ cup of the reserved poaching liquid until smooth. Add chicken and toss well.

4 Whisk the vegetable oil, the remaining 2 tablespoons soy sauce, and the remaining ½ teaspoon sesame oil in a large bowl.

5 Cook the pasta according to package directions. Rinse under cold water and drain. Toss with soy sauce mixture. Arrange on a platter and top with julienned chicken and vegetables. Sprinkle with sesame seed. Makes 4 servings.

PER SERVING		DAILY GOAL	
Calories	480	2,000 (F), 2,500 (M)	
Total Fat	17 g	60 g or less (F), 70 g or less (M)	
Saturated fat	2 g	20 g or less (F), 23 g or less (M)	
Cholesterol	141 mg	300 mg or less	
Sodium	1,444 mg	2,400 mg or less	
Carbohydrates	45 g	250 g or more	
Protein	38 g	55 g to 90 g	

NOTES

CITRUS CHICKEN STIR-FRY WITH SPRING VEGETABLES

Here's an updated version of your favorite sweet-and-sour stir-fry. Fresh lemon, rice vinegar, and just a touch of sugar are perfect with the tender strips of chicken and crisp-tender veggies.

▽ *Low-calorie*
   Prep time: 15 minutes
   Cooking time: 5 minutes
○ *Degree of difficulty: easy*

2 **tablespoons reduced-sodium soy sauce**
1 **tablespoon dry sherry**
1 **tablespoon cornstarch**
1 **pound boneless, skinless chicken breasts, cut into ½-inch thick strips**
¼ **cup fresh lemon juice**
2 **tablespoons rice wine vinegar**
1 **tablespoon sugar**
1 **teaspoon grated lemon peel**
2 **tablespoons vegetable oil, divided**

½ **pound asparagus, cut into ¾-inch pieces**
1 **tablespoon water**
1 **bunch watercress (1½ cups), trimmed**
2 **green onions, sliced**
1 **teaspoon grated fresh ginger**
1 **teaspoon minced garlic**

1 For marinade, combine the soy sauce, sherry, and cornstarch in medium bowl; blend until smooth. Add the chicken and toss to coat.

2 Combine the lemon juice, vinegar, sugar, and lemon peel in another bowl; set aside.

3 Heat 1 tablespoon of the oil in a large skillet or wok over medium-high heat. Add the asparagus and water; stir-fry for 30 seconds. Add the watercress, green onions, ginger, and garlic. Stir-fry until watercress is just wilted, about 1 minute more. Transfer to a plate; keep warm.

4 Increase heat to high. Add the remaining 1 tablespoon oil to skillet. Add chicken with marinade; stir-fry until just cooked through, about 3 minutes. Stir in the lemon mixture and simmer for 1 minute more. Stir in vegetables. Makes 4 servings.

PER SERVING		DAILY GOAL
Calories	240	2,000 (F), 2,500 (M)
Total Fat	8 g	60 g or less (F), 70 g or less (M)
Saturated fat	1 g	20 g or less (F), 23 g or less (M)
Cholesterol	66 mg	300 mg or less
Sodium	383 mg	2,400 mg or less
Carbohydrates	11 g	250 g or more
Protein	29 g	55 g to 90 g

NOTES

_____

_____

_____

_____

_____

_____

_____

_____

_____

_____

_____

_____

_____

_____

CHINESE CHICKEN NOODLE SOUP

Enjoy the cozy comfort of a homemade chicken soup with an Oriental twist. Make the stock a day ahead and skim off the fat.

▼ *Low-fat*
▽ *Low-calorie*
   Prep time: 1¼ hours plus chilling
   Cooking time: 25 minutes
○ *Degree of difficulty: easy*

1 **chicken (3 pounds), cut up**
1 **can (13¾ or 14½ ounces) chicken broth**
6 **cups water**
1 **cup chopped onions**
3 **whole garlic cloves**
½ **teaspoon salt**
½ **teaspoon red pepper flakes**
½ **pound mushrooms (3 cups), sliced**
¼ **pound snow peas (2 cups), trimmed and sliced lengthwise**
1 **cup shredded carrots**
2 **tablespoons soy sauce**
1 **tablespoon grated fresh ginger**
½ **teaspoon Oriental sesame oil**

1 **package (9 ounces) fresh angel hair pasta**
½ **cup diagonally sliced green onions**
¼ **cup chopped fresh cilantro**

1 For stock, combine the chicken, chicken broth, water, onions, garlic, salt, and red pepper flakes in a Dutch oven. Bring just to a boil. Reduce heat and simmer gently, 45 minutes. Drain, reserving broth and chicken separately.

2 Cool chicken slightly. Remove meat from bones and dice; cover and refrigerate. Freeze broth for 1 hour or refrigerate overnight; skim fat.

3 Return broth to Dutch oven and bring to a boil. Add the chicken, mushrooms, snow peas, carrots, soy sauce, ginger, and sesame oil. Return to a boil. Add the pasta and green onions. Cook, stirring, 2 minutes. Sprinkle with cilantro. Makes 10 cups.

PER SERVING		DAILY GOAL	
Calories	185	2,000 (F), 2,500 (M)	
Total Fat	3 g	60 g or less (F), 70 g or less (M)	
Saturated fat	1 g	20 g or less (F), 23 g or less (M)	
Cholesterol	76 mg	300 mg or less	
Sodium	583 mg	2,400 mg or less	
Carbohydrates	19 g	250 g or more	
Protein	19 g	55 g to 90 g	

VIETNAMESE CHICKEN BUNDLES

Vietnamese cuisine has roots in many cultures, including Indian, French, and Chinese. The emphasis is always on freshness. Here grilled chicken is rolled up piping hot in crisp lettuce leaves and served with a piquant dipping sauce.

▽   *Low-calorie*
    Prep time: 35 minutes plus standing
    Cooking time: 8 minutes

○   *Degree of difficulty: easy*

3   **tablespoons Oriental fish sauce (nuoc mam) *or* soy sauce**
5   **tablespoons water, divided**
4   **teaspoons sugar, divided**
1   **teaspoon minced garlic**
1   **pound boneless, skinless chicken thighs, cut into 1½-inch cubes**
1   **medium onion, cut in wedges and separated into layers**
1   **tablespoon grated carrot**
2   **teaspoons rice wine vinegar, divided**
10 **pearl onions (3 ounces), peeled**
2   **carrots, sliced thin**
2   **heads leaf lettuce**
    Mint sprigs
1   **cucumber, sliced thin**
¼   **chopped peanuts, for garnish**
2   **tablespoons chopped green onions, for garnish**

1 Soak 8 bamboo skewers in water for at least 30 minutes. Preheat the grill or broiler and broiler pan. If grilling, prepare grill for direct heat.

2 Mix the fish sauce, 2 tablespoons of the water, 1 teaspoon of the sugar, and garlic in small bowl. Skewer the chicken and onion wedges; place in shallow dish. Pour 3 tablespoons of sauce over chicken. Add remaining 3 tablespoons water, the grated carrot, and 1 teaspoon of the sugar to remaining sauce in bowl for dipping.

3 Place 1 teaspoon of rice wine vinegar and 1 teaspoon sugar in each of 2 small bowls.

4 Bring 2 inches of water to a boil in each of 2 small saucepans. Add the pearl onions to 1 pan and cook until soft, about 6 minutes; drain. Toss with vinegar mixture in one of the bowls. Cook carrots in the other saucepan until tender-crisp, about 1 minute; drain. Place in second bowl; toss.

5 Cook chicken 4 inches from heat source, 4 minutes per side or until firm. Arrange on a platter with lettuce, mint, carrots, pearl onions, and cucumber. Serve with dipping sauce. Makes 4 servings.

PER SERVING		DAILY GOAL
Calories	300	2,000 (F), 2,500 (M)
Total Fat	11 g	60 g or less (F), 70 g or less (M)
Saturated fat	2 g	20 g or less (F), 23 g or less (M)
Cholesterol	94 mg	300 mg or less
Sodium	127 mg	2,400 mg or less
Carbohydrates	24 g	250 g or more
Protein	30 g	55 g to 90 g

NOTES

_____

_____

_____

_____

_____

_____

_____

_____

STIR-FRY LIME CHICKEN

Stir-frying is one of the fastest ways to cook chicken; the secret is to make sure the oil is very hot. Fresh lime juice and lime peel give an unusual twist to this low calorie entrée.

▽ *Low-calorie*
Prep time: 10 minutes plus marinating
Cooking time: 7 minutes
○ *Degree of difficulty: easy*

3 **tablespoons fresh lime juice**
2 **tablespoons soy sauce**
1 **teaspoon minced garlic**
1 **teaspoon minced jalapeño chili**
½ **teaspoon grated lime peel**
½ **teaspoon grated fresh ginger**
4 **boneless, skinless chicken breast halves (about 1 pound), cut into 1-inch pieces**
1 **teaspoon cornstarch**
2 **tablespoons vegetable oil, divided**
2 **medium zucchini, julienned**
½ **red pepper julienned**
½ **yellow pepper julienned**
¼ **teaspoon salt**
¼ **teaspoon freshly ground pepper**

1 Combine the lime juice, soy sauce, garlic, jalapeño, lime peel, and ginger in a large glass bowl. Add the chicken, then cornstarch and toss to coat. Cover and refrigerate 1 hour.

2 Heat 1 tablespoon of the oil in a large skillet or wok over medium-high heat. Add the zucchini, red and yellow pepper, salt, and pepper. Stir-fry until tender-crisp, about 2 minutes. Transfer to a plate.

3 Heat remaining 1 tablespoon oil in the same skillet. Add chicken. Stir-fry until opaque and firm to the touch, about 3 to 5 minutes. Return vegetables to skillet; cook, stirring, until heated through, for 30 seconds more. Makes 4 servings.

PER SERVING		DAILY GOAL
Calories	215	2,000 (F), 2,500 (M)
Total Fat	8 g	60 g or less (F), 70 g or less (M)
Saturated fat	1 g	20 g or less (F), 23 g or less (M)
Cholesterol	66 mg	300 mg or less
Sodium	727 mg	2,400 mg or less
Carbohydrates	6 g	250 g or more
Protein	28 g	55 g to 90 g

47

PACIFIC RIM CHICKEN POCKETS

Pacific Rim cooking is a trendy mix of flavors, textures, and techniques from Asian and Western cultures. Serve this light entrée with a watercress salad.

▼ *Low-fat*
▽ *Low-calorie*
   Prep time: 20 minutes plus marinating
   Cooking time: 8 minutes
○ *Degree of difficulty: easy*

- 2 **tablespoons soy sauce**
- 4 **tablespoons balsamic vinegar, divided**
- 1 **teaspoon grated fresh ginger**
- 1 **teaspoon minced garlic**
- ¼ **teaspoon freshly ground pepper**
- 4 **boneless, skinless chicken breast halves (about 1 pound)**
- 2 **tablespoons hoisin sauce**
- 8 **small (6-inch) flour tortillas**
- 2 **cups julienned jicama**
- 2 **cups julienned carrots**
- 8 **green onions, julienned**

1 Combine the soy sauce, 2 tablespoons of the vinegar, ginger, garlic, and pepper in a medium bowl. Add the chicken breast halves; toss to coat. Cover and refrigerate for 1 hour.

2 Preheat the broiler. Combine the hoisin sauce and the remaining 2 tablespoons vinegar in a cup.

3 Broil chicken 3 inches from heat source for 3 to 4 minutes per side, until it is opaque in the center. On a cutting board, slice each breast half lengthwise into ½-inch-thick strips.

4 For each pocket, spread 1 side of a tortilla with 1 teaspoon of the hoisin mixture. Place half of one sliced chicken breast in the center and top with ¼ cup each jicama, carrot, and green onion. Roll tortilla up over filling. Repeat to make 7 more rolls. Makes 4 servings.

PER SERVING		DAILY GOAL	
Calories	330	2,000 (F), 2,500 (M)	
Total Fat	5 g	60 g or less (F), 70 g or less (M)	
Saturated fat	1 g	20 g or less (F), 23 g or less (M)	
Cholesterol	66 mg	300 mg or less	
Sodium	1,062 mg	2,400 mg or less	
Carbohydrates	39 g	250 g or more	
Protein	33 g	55 g to 90 g	

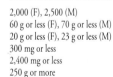

NOTES

_____
_____
_____
_____
_____
_____
_____
_____
_____
_____
_____
_____
_____
_____
_____
_____
_____
_____
_____

CHICKEN PALERMO WITH SWEET SAUSAGE

This skillet supper bursts with the hearty flavors of southern Italy. To help reduce fat, cook the meats separately and drain off the drippings.

▽ *Low-calorie*
  Prep time: 10 minutes
  Cooking time: 50 to 60 minutes
○ *Degree of difficulty: easy*

½ **pound sweet Italian sausages**
6 **chicken thighs (1½ to 2 pounds)**
½ **teaspoon salt**
¼ **teaspoon freshly ground pepper**
1 **onion, chopped**
1 **teaspoon minced garlic**
½ **teaspoon rosemary, crushed**
½ **cup chicken broth**
1 **tablespoon red wine vinegar**

1 Prick the sausage all over with a fork. Cook in a large skillet over medium heat until browned on all sides and cooked through, 10 to 15 minutes. Drain on paper towels; discard the drippings from pan.

2 Sprinkle the chicken with salt and pepper. Add chicken to a skillet, skin side down; cook until browned on all sides, about 8 minutes. Remove chicken from pan; discard drippings.

3 Add the onion to skillet and cook until tender, about 5 minutes. Stir in the garlic and rosemary; cook for 10 seconds. Add the broth and vinegar. Cut sausages in thirds and return to skillet with chicken. Simmer covered for 25 to 30 minutes. Makes 6 servings.

PER SERVING		DAILY GOAL	
Calories	275	2,000 (F), 2,500 (M)	
Total Fat	18 g	60 g or less (F), 70 g or less (M)	
Saturated fat	6 g	20 g or less (F), 23 g or less (M)	
Cholesterol	85 mg	300 mg or less	
Sodium	592 mg	2,400 mg or less	
Carbohydrates	3 g	250 g or more	
Protein	23 g	55 g to 90 g	

NOTES

PROSCIUTTO-WRAPPED CHICKEN WITH SAGE

Ready when you are, these chicken breasts filled with a fragrant herb butter and, then wrapped in smoky prosciutto ham, can be prepared a day ahead. Simply pop them in the oven when your guests arrive.

▽ *Low-calorie*
Prep time: 30 minutes
Cooking time: 25 to 30 minutes
● *Degree of difficulty: moderate*

6 **tablespoons butter**
(no substitutions), softened
1 **tablespoon chopped fresh sage**
½ **teaspoon minced garlic**
¼ **teaspoon salt**
8 **boneless, skinless chicken breast**
halves (about 2 pounds)
8 **slices prosciutto ham**
Freshly ground pepper
1 **tablespoon olive oil**

1 Preheat oven to 375°F. Combine the butter, sage, garlic, and salt in a small bowl. With a small, sharp knife cut a pocket in the thicker side of each chicken breast half. Spread 2 teaspoons of butter mixture in each pocket. Wrap each chicken breast in 1 slice of the prosciutto.

2 Place chicken breasts in a 13x9-inch baking pan. Sprinkle with pepper and brush with oil. Cover pan with foil. (Can be made ahead. Refrigerate up to 24 hours.)

3 Bake for 20 to 25 minutes or until chicken is firm to the touch. Remove foil and bake for 5 minutes more. Makes 8 servings.

PER SERVING		DAILY GOAL
Calories	280	2,000 (F), 2,500 (M)
Total Fat	16 g	60 g or less (F), 70 g or less (M)
Saturated fat	7 g	20 g or less (F), 23 g or less (M)
Cholesterol	112 mg	300 mg or less
Sodium	753 mg	2,400 mg or less
Carbohydrates	0 g	250 g or more
Protein	34 g	55 g to 90 g

51

CHICKEN ALLA PANNA ROSA

There's no substitute for the flavor of fresh basil in this quick tomato and cream sauce with a rosy-pink hue.

▽ *Low-calorie*
Prep time: 15 to 20 minutes
Cooking time: 20 minutes
○ *Degree of difficulty: easy*

1 **tablespoon butter *or* margarine**
½ **cup finely chopped onion**
1 **can (14 ounces) plum tomatoes, coarsely chopped**
½ **cup heavy *or* whipping cream**
½ **cup julienned fresh basil leaves**
½ **teaspoon salt**
½ **teaspoon freshly ground pepper**
6 **boneless, skinless chicken breast halves (about 1½ pounds)**

1 Preheat oven to 450°F. Heat the butter in a skillet over medium heat. Add the onion and cook until translucent, about 5 minutes. Increase heat to high; add the tomatoes and cook until liquid is almost evaporated, for 5 to 10 minutes. Add the cream and bring to a boil; boil until slightly thickened, about 3 minutes. Stir in the basil, salt, and pepper.

2 Arrange the chicken in a shallow baking dish; pour sauce on top. Bake for 20 minutes. Makes 6 servings.

PER SERVING		DAILY GOAL
Calories	230	2,000 (F), 2,500 (M)
Total Fat	11 g	60 g or less (F), 70 g or less (M)
Saturated fat	6 g	20 g or less (F), 23 g or less (M)
Cholesterol	98 mg	300 mg or less
Sodium	392 mg	2,400 mg or less
Carbohydrates	5 g	250 g or more
Protein	28 g	55 g to 90 g

NOTES

CHICKEN MARSALA

Marsala is Italy's most famous fortified wine. It is available in both sweet and dry varieties. Either variety has a deep, smoky flavor which is perfect in this sauce enriched with fresh mushrooms and sage.

▼ *Low-fat*
▽ *Low-calorie*
  Prep time: 10 minutes
  Cooking time: 20 to 25 minutes
○ *Degree of difficulty: easy*

  4 **boneless, skinless chicken-breast halves (1 pound)**
  ½ **teaspoon salt**
  ¼ **teaspoon freshly ground pepper**
  ¼ **teaspoon sage**
  1 **teaspoon vegetable oil**
  ½ **cup finely chopped onion**
  ½ **pound mushrooms (3 cups), sliced**
  ¼ **cup Marsala wine**
  ½ **cup chicken broth**
  1 **tablespoon minced fresh parsley**

1 Sprinkle both sides of the chicken with salt, pepper, and sage. Heat the oil in a large nonstick skillet over medium-high heat. Add chicken and cook until golden, about 4 minutes per side. Transfer to a serving plate and keep warm.

2 Add the onion to skillet and cook, stirring, until tender, for 3 to 5 minutes. Add the mushrooms and cook, stirring, for 5 minutes more. Stir in the wine and chicken broth. Bring to a boil and cook until reduced by half, about 5 minutes. Pour over chicken and sprinkle with parsley. Makes 4 servings.

PER SERVING		DAILY GOAL	
Calories	185	2,000 (F), 2,500 (M)	
Total Fat	3 g	60 g or less (F), 70 g or less (M)	
Saturated fat	1 g	20 g or less (F), 23 g or less (M)	
Cholesterol	66	300 mg or less	
Sodium	497 mg	2,400 mg or less	
Carbohydrates	6 g	250 g or more	
Protein	28 g	55 g to 90 g	

A-B-C-DEGLAZE

Deglazing is one of the easiest and most flavorful ways to make sauces for chicken, a flash-in-the-pan technique worth learning. Here's how:

Cook chicken as directed in a skillet and transfer it to a warm serving platter. Carefully, pour a small amount of flavorful liquid like wine, lemon juice, flavored vinegar, or chicken broth (or any combination) into the hot skillet. Cook over high heat, scraping up any browned bits from the bottom of the pan with a wooden spoon. Continue cooking until the sauce is reduced and syrupy. For extra richness, remove the skillet from the heat and whisk in a tablespoon or two of room-temperature butter until it is melted. Pour the sauce over cooked chicken and serve immediately.

STUFFED CHICKEN BREASTS FLORENTINE

Here's an elegant stuffed chicken dish ready in less than an hour. Be sure to remove the tough spinach stems before cooking.

Prep time: 25 minutes
Cooking time: 20 minutes
○ *Degree of difficulty: easy*

6 cups (6 ounces) fresh spinach
2 tablespoons butter *or* margarine
½ cup chopped onion
½ cup chopped fresh mushrooms
¼ cup freshly grated Parmesan cheese
Salt
Freshly ground pepper
⅛ teaspoon nutmeg
Pinch ground red pepper
2 chicken breasts (2½ pounds), split
2 tablespoons vegetable oil

1 Preheat oven to 450°F. Wash the spinach. Place in a large skillet; cover and cook in the water clinging to the leaves just until wilted. Drain, squeeze dry, and chop.

2 In same skillet melt the butter over medium-high heat. Add the onion and sauté until translucent, about 5 minutes. Add the mushrooms and cook for 2 minutes more.

3 Transfer to a medium bowl with spinach, Parmesan, ¼ teaspoon each of salt and pepper, nutmeg, and red pepper; mix well.

4 Spread spinach mixture under the skin of each chicken breast. Sprinkle chicken with salt and pepper.

5 Add the oil to skillet; heat over medium-high heat. Add chicken skin side down and cook until golden, about 3 to 5 minutes. Turn chicken and cook for 1 to 2 minutes more. Transfer to baking dish and bake 20 minutes. Makes 4 servings.

PER SERVING		DAILY GOAL
Calories	455	2,000 (F), 2,500 (M)
Total Fat	26 g	60 g or less (F), 70 g or less (M)
Saturated fat	9 g	20 g or less (F), 23 g or less (M)
Cholesterol	148 mg	300 mg or less
Sodium	295 mg	2,400 mg or less
Carbohydrates	3 g	250 g or more
Protein	49 g	55 g to 90 g

NOTES

CHICKEN CACCIATORE

"Cacciatore" means hunter's style, and this classic chicken dish from Italy always includes tomatoes, onions, and wine. We've added slow-cooked sweet bell peppers and garlic to give the sauce extra rich flavor.

Prep time: 45 minutes
Cooking time: 50 to 60 minutes
○ *Degree of difficulty: easy*

1 **chicken (4 pounds), cut up**
2 **tablespoons vegetable oil, divided**
2 **green peppers, cored, seeded and sliced into strips**
4 **medium onions (1½ pounds), sliced**
1 **tablespoon minced garlic**
1 **can (15 ounces) whole tomatoes**
¼ **cup dry red wine**
¼ **cup chopped fresh basil**
1 **teaspoon salt**
½ **teaspoon oregano**
½ **teaspoon freshly ground pepper**
1 **pound fresh mushrooms, quartered**

1 Preheat oven to 350°F. In a large Dutch oven heat 1 tablespoon of the oil over medium-high heat. Add half the chicken and brown on both sides, about 7 minutes per side. Remove chicken and transfer to a plate. Repeat with remaining chicken.

2 Discard all but 1 tablespoon of drippings from Dutch oven. Stir in the peppers, onions, and garlic. Cook over medium heat stirring occasionally until peppers are soft and onions are translucent, about 15 minutes. Add the tomatoes, wine, basil, salt, oregano, pepper, and chicken to the pot. Bring to a boil. Cover and transfer to oven. Bake for 50 to 60 minutes or until chicken is tender.

3 In a large skillet, heat the remaining 1 tablespoon oil over medium-high heat. Add the mushrooms and cook until liquid has evaporated, about 4 minutes. Stir the mushrooms into sauce mixture in Dutch oven. Makes 6 servings.

PER SERVING		DAILY GOAL
Calories	550	2,000 (F), 2,500 (M)
Total Fat	34 g	60 g or less (F), 70 g or less (M)
Saturated fat	9 g	20 g or less (F), 23 g or less (M)
Cholesterol	154 mg	300 mg or less
Sodium	634 mg	2,400 mg or less
Carbohydrates	19 g	250 g or more
Protein	42 g	55 g to 90 g

BISTRO-ROASTED CHICKEN

Here's classic French country fare. This crispy chicken for two includes a wonderful roasted garlic sauce, which is sublime with your favorite mashed potatoes!

Prep time: 5 minutes plus standing
Cooking time: 45 minutes
○ *Degree of difficulty: easy*

1 **small whole chicken (2 to 2½ pounds)**
1 **tablespoon butter *or* margarine, softened**
¾ **teaspoon coarse *or* kosher salt**
½ **teaspoon freshly ground pepper**
¼ **teaspoon thyme**
1 **small head garlic**
¼ **cup plus 2 tablespoons chicken broth**
¼ **cup white wine**

1 Remove the chicken from refrigerator 30 minutes before roasting. Preheat oven to 450°F. Rinse chicken under cold water and dry thoroughly. Rub all over with the butter.

2 Place in a cast-iron skillet; sprinkle with salt, pepper, and thyme. Roast for 35 to 40 minutes, until juices run clear when the chicken is pierced with a fork or a meat thermometer inserted in the thigh reaches 180°F.

3 Meanwhile, peel off the outer skin of the garlic and place head in a small ramekin with the 2 tablespoons chicken broth. Cover tightly and roast 40 minutes.

4 Transfer chicken to a platter; keep warm. Add the wine and the remaining ¼ cup broth to skillet and boil over high heat for 2 minutes, scraping up any browned bits. Skim fat and discard.

5 Squeeze the garlic cloves from skins and press through a sieve. Whisk into pan juices. Cut chicken in half. Serve with pan juices. Makes 2 servings.

PER SERVING		DAILY GOAL
Calories	780	2,000 (F), 2,500 (M)
Total Fat	44 g	60 g or less (F), 70 g or less (M)
Saturated fat	14 g	20 g or less (F), 23 g or less (M)
Cholesterol	257 mg	300 mg or less
Sodium	1,060 mg	2,400 mg or less
Carbohydrates	11 g	250 g or more
Protein	77 g	55 g to 90 g

A CARVING PRIMER: STEP BY STEP

Carving a whole chicken is easier than you think. For the best results, use a long, sharp knife and a long-pronged fork. Work on one side of the bird at a time. The trick is to cut off the thigh, wings and drumstick first—that makes slicing the breast a breeze.

If your chicken is stuffed, transfer the stuffing to a serving dish before carving and place the chicken on a carving board. Insert a long fork into the top of the breast bone to hold the chicken firmly in place. To remove the drumstick and thigh, grasp the drumstick and pull the whole leg away from the body. If the joint does not just snap free, insert a knife point into the joint and twist the blade slightly. Following the body contour carefully, cut away the dark meat at the joint area. Place the thigh and drumstick on the cutting surface and cut through the connecting joint to separate. Set the pieces aside on a warm serving platter.

To slice the chicken breast, cut and remove the first two joints of the wing and transfer them to the serving platter, leaving the third joint attached to the bird. Place the knife parallel and as close to the remaining wing joint as possible. Make a deep cut into the breast towards the ribs. (Each breast slice will stop at this horizontal base cut.) Carve the breast downward toward the base, cutting in thin, even slices; transfer to the warm platter. Repeat the process on other side of the chicken.

Do Ahead Tip: To keep your chicken and stuffing hot and super moist after carving, arrange the slices on an oven-proof platter and the stuffing in an oven-proof bowl. Place in a preheated 200°F. oven; drizzle both with warm chicken stock and cover loosely with foil. They will stay moist up to 20 minutes.

Tip: After carving the chicken, pieces can be broiled briefly to reheat and crisp the skin.

CHICKEN SAUTÉ PROVENÇALE

This is a quick robust dish using the traditional flavorings of southern France—olives, capers, anchovies, and tomatoes.

▽ *Low-calorie*
  Prep time: 5 minutes
  Cooking time: 18 minutes
○ *Degree of difficulty: easy*

1 **tablespoon olive oil**
4 **boneless, skinless chicken breast halves (about 1 pound)**
½ **teaspoon salt**
½ **teaspoon freshly ground pepper**
½ **cup chopped onion**
2 **teaspoons minced garlic**
3 **flat anchovy fillets, chopped**
1 **can (14 ounces) plum tomatoes**
2 **tablespoons Niçoise *or* Greek olives, pitted**
1 **tablespoon chopped fresh parsley**
2 **teaspoons capers**

1 Heat the oil in a large skillet over medium-high heat. Pat the chicken dry; sprinkle with salt and pepper. Add to skillet and cook until golden and firm to the touch, about 3 to 4 minutes per side. Transfer to serving dish and keep warm.

2 Reduce heat to medium. Add the onion to skillet and cook until softened, about 5 minutes. Stir in the garlic and anchovies and cook for 30 seconds. Add the tomatoes, breaking them up with a spoon; cook over high heat until thickened, about 5 minutes. Stir in the olives, parsley, and capers and spoon over chicken. Makes 4 servings.

PER SERVING		DAILY GOAL
Calories	205	2,000 (F), 2,500 (M)
Total Fat	7 g	60 g or less (F), 70 g or less (M)
Saturated fat	1 g	20 g or less (F), 23 g or less (M)
Cholesterol	68 mg	300 mg or less
Sodium	805 mg	2,400 mg or less
Carbohydrates	7 g	250 g or more
Protein	29 g	55 g to 90 g

NOTES

CHICKEN WITH PANCETTA AND ZINFANDEL

Here's a California-style variation on the French classic, Coq au Vin. Wonderful for entertaining, it can be prepared, covered, and refrigerated up to two days ahead. Just reheat it in a Dutch oven over medium heat, stirring occasionally, until hot.

Prep time: 50 minutes
Cooking time: 45 minutes
Degree of difficulty: moderate

- 4 **ounces pancetta, prosciutto ham, *or* bacon, cut into ½-inch cubes**
- 4 **tablespoons butter *or* margarine, divided**
- 1 **chicken (4 pounds), cut into 10 pieces**
- ¼ **teaspoon salt**
- ¼ **cup finely chopped shallots**
- ¼ **cup all-purpose flour**
- 3 **cups zinfandel *or* dry red wine**
- 1½ **cups chicken broth, divided**
- ¼ **teaspoon thyme**
- ½ **bay leaf**
- 10 **ounces pearl onions, peeled**
- 1 **pound small fresh mushrooms, trimmed**
- 2 **tablespoons chopped fresh parsley**

1 Preheat oven to 325°F. In a medium saucepan blanch the pancetta or bacon in boiling water for 1 minute; drain. (Prosciutto does not need to be blanched.) Cook pancetta, bacon, or prosciutto in a large skillet over low heat with 1 tablespoon of the butter until crisp and golden brown. Transfer to a bowl.

2 Increase heat to medium-high. Cook the chicken in 2 batches, turning occasionally, until brown on all sides, about 10 minutes. Remove chicken to a 5-quart Dutch oven. Sprinkle with the pancetta and salt.

3 Pour off all but 2 tablespoons of drippings from the skillet. Add the shallots and sauté for 5 minutes. Sprinkle with the flour and cook, stirring, for 1 minute. Slowly whisk in the wine. Add 1 cup of the chicken broth, thyme, and bay leaf; boil for 5 minutes. Pour into Dutch oven. Wipe out skillet.

4 Melt 1 tablespoon of the butter in the same skillet over medium-high heat. Add the onions and sauté until browned, for 5 minutes. Add the remaining ½ cup of chicken broth; cover, and cook until liquid is almost evaporated, about 4 minutes. Add to Dutch oven; bring to a boil. Cover and bake for 35 minutes.

5 Meanwhile, melt the remaining 2 tablespoons of butter in a large skillet over medium-high heat. Add the mushrooms and saute until golden, about 5 minutes. Add to Dutch oven and cook for 10 minutes more. Sprinkle with parsley before serving. Makes 6 servings.

PER SERVING		DAILY GOAL	
Calories	590	2,000 (F), 2,500 (M)	
Total Fat	38 g	60 g or less (F), 70 g or less (M)	
Saturated fat	12 g	20 g or less (F), 23 g or less (M)	
Cholesterol	180 mg	300 mg or less	
Sodium	927 mg	2,400 mg or less	
Carbohydrates	13 g	250 g or more	
Protein	47 g	55 g to 90 g	

NOTES

_____

_____

_____

_____

_____

CHICKEN NORMANDY

This classic entrée, inspired by the cuisine of northern France, features a sophisticated combination of pears and tarragon.

Prep time: 5 minutes
Cooking time: 15 to 18 minutes
Degree of difficulty: easy

1 **tablespoon vegetable oil**
4 **boneless, skinless chicken breast halves (about 1 pound)**
   Salt
   Freshly ground pepper
1 **tablespoon butter *or* margarine**
½ **cup finely chopped onion**
2 **ripe pears, cut into 8 wedges each**
3 **tablespoons cognac *or* brandy**
½ **cup heavy *or* whipping cream**
½ **teaspoon dried tarragon**

1 Heat the oil in a large skillet over medium-high heat. Pat the chicken breasts dry on paper towels; sprinkle with salt and pepper. Add to skillet and cook until just firm, about 5 minutes per side. Remove from skillet; keep warm.

2 Melt the butter in the same skillet over medium-high heat. Add the onion and pears. Cover and cook, stirring occasionally, until pears are tender and golden, about 3 to 5 minutes. Add the cognac; cook uncovered until almost all of the liquid is evaporated, about 30 seconds. Stir in the cream, tarragon, and ¼ teaspoon each of salt and pepper. Cook over high heat until sauce is thickened, about 3 minutes. Spoon over chicken. Makes 4 servings.

PER SERVING		DAILY GOAL
Calories	370	2,000 (F), 2,500 (M)
Total Fat	19 g	60 g or less (F), 70 g or less (M)
Saturated fat	9.5 g	20 g or less (F), 23 g or less (M)
Cholesterol	114 mg	300 mg or less
Sodium	250 mg	2,400 mg or less
Carbohydrates	15 g	250 g or more
Protein	27 g	55 g to 90 g

NOTES

61

CHICKEN FROM
THE BORDER

We rounded up your favorite Tex-Mex burritos, enchiladas and tostadas and chicken loves them all. So chow down on some Southwest Chicken Burgers with green chilies, Arroz con Pollo, or Chicken Tamales and don't forget to pass the salsa.

QUICK CHICKEN BURRITOS

This is an ideal entrée to prepare when your family can't eat dinner together. You can make all the filling at once, then roll up each burrito as needed.

Prep time: 25 minutes
Baking time: 5 minutes
○ *Degree of difficulty: easy*

2 **tablespoons vegetable oil**
1 **pound boneless, skinless chicken breasts, cut into ¼-inch strips**
½ **teaspoon salt**
¼ **teaspoon freshly ground pepper**
   Half of 1 medium onion, sliced thin
1 **teaspoon minced garlic**
1 **teaspoon cumin**
   Half of 1 green pepper, sliced thin
2 **fresh plum tomatoes, sliced thin**
2 **tablespoons canned chopped green chilies**
¼ **cup fresh cilantro leaves**
1 **can (15 ounces) pinto beans, drained, rinsed, and mashed**
4 **large (10-inch) flour tortillas**

1¼ **cups shredded pepper-jack cheese, divided**
   Salsa and sour cream, for garnish

1 Preheat oven to 375°F. Heat the oil in a large skillet over high heat. Add the chicken, salt, and pepper; cook, stirring occasionally, until cooked through, about 4 minutes. With a slotted spoon, transfer to a plate; keep warm.

2 Add the onion, garlic, and cumin to drippings in skillet; cook until fragrant, about 1 minute. Add the green pepper, tomatoes, and green chilies; cook, stirring, until tender, about 3 minutes. Return chicken to skillet; add the cilantro and heat through.

3 Spread the beans evenly down the center of tortillas. Top each with ¾ cup of the chicken filling; sprinkle with ¼ cup of the cheese. Fold bottom third of each tortilla over filling. Fold sides over filling; roll up tightly.

4 Place burritos seam side down in a shallow 13x9-inch baking dish. Sprinkle with the remaining ¼ cup cheese. Cover with foil. Bake 5 minutes. Serve with salsa and sour cream. Makes 4 servings.

PER SERVING WITHOUT GARNISHES		DAILY GOAL
Calories	510	2,000 (F), 2,500 (M)
Total Fat	20 g	60 g or less (F), 70 g or less (M)
Saturated fat	8 g	20 g or less (F), 23 g or less (M)
Cholesterol	103 mg	300 mg or less
Sodium	995 mg	2,400 mg or less
Carbohydrates	38 g	250 g or more
Protein	43 g	55 g to 90 g

NOTES

GRILLED CHICKEN FAJITAS

The chicken only needs an hour to marinate in this zesty Southwestern combo featuring Salsa Cruda and Guacamole.

▼ *Low-fat*
Prep time: 30 minutes plus marinating
Cooking time: 8 to 10 minutes
O *Degree of difficulty: easy*

½ **cup fresh lime juice**
2 **teaspoons minced garlic**
1 **teaspoon red pepper flakes**
2 **pounds boneless, skinless chicken breasts**
Salt
12 **large (10-inch) flour tortillas**

Salsa Cruda
6 **fresh plum tomatoes, diced**
½ **cup minced red onions**
¼ **cup chopped fresh cilantro**
2 **jalapeño chilies, minced**
1 **teaspoon salt**

Guacamole
2 **ripe avocados, peeled and pitted**
¼ **cup minced red onions**

2 **tablespoons fresh lime juice**
½ **teaspoon salt**
¼ **teaspoon red pepper sauce**

1 Combine the lime juice, garlic, and red pepper flakes in a glass bowl. Add the chicken; cover and refrigerate, turning occasionally, for 1 hour.

2 Prepare the grill. Remove chicken from marinade; sprinkle with salt.

3 Grill 3 inches from the heat source 4 to 5 minutes per side, until opaque in the center. Slice and serve with warm tortillas, Salsa Cruda and Guacamole. Makes 6 servings.

Salsa Cruda: Combine the tomatoes, red onions, cilantro, jalapeño chilies, and salt in a glass bowl. Makes 3 cups.

Guacamole: Mash the avocados, red onions, lime juice, salt, and red pepper sauce in a bowl with a potato masher or large fork. Makes 2 cups.

PER SERVING		DAILY GOAL
Calories	530	2,000 (F), 2,500 (M)
Total Fat	13 g	60 g or less (F), 70 g or less (M)
Saturated fat	2 g	20 g or less (F), 23 g or less (M)
Cholesterol	88 mg	300 mg or less
Sodium	1,082 mg	2,400 mg or less
Carbohydrates	59 g	250 g or more
Protein	44 g	55 g to 90 g

65

RELLENO-STUFFED CHICKEN WITH BLACK BEANS AND CREAMY CILANTRO DRESSING

We've removed the bone from this stuffed chicken breast, but left the skin on for extra moistness and flavor. *Also pictured on page 62.*

Prep time: 30 minutes
Cooking time: 25 to 30 minutes
● *Degree of difficulty: moderate*

1½ **cups shredded Monterey jack cheese**
3 **tablespoons minced green onions**
4 **teaspoons minced fresh cilantro**
1 **teaspoon minced garlic**
¾ **teaspoon cumin**
8 **boneless chicken breast halves with skin (about 3½ pounds)**
4 **teaspoons olive oil**
½ **teaspoon salt**
½ **teaspoon freshly ground pepper**
  Small romaine lettuce leaves

Black Bean Salad
3 **cans (15 ounces each) black beans, rinsed and drained**
4 **plum tomatoes, seeded and chopped (2 cups)**
2 **avocados, peeled, pitted, and diced**
½ **cup sliced green onions**
2 **tablespoons fresh lime juice**
1 **tablespoon vegetable oil**
½ **teaspoon cumin**
½ **teaspoon salt**
¼ **teaspoon freshly ground pepper**

Creamy Cilantro Dressing
2 **cups lightly packed fresh cilantro leaves *or* 2 cups fresh parsley plus 2 tablespoons dried cilantro**
1 **cup sour cream**
½ **cup mayonnaise**
2 **tablespoons fresh lime juice**
¼ **teaspoon minced garlic**
¼ **teaspoon grated lime peel**

1 Preheat oven to 425°F. Combine cheese, green onions, cilantro, garlic, and cumin in a bowl. Loosen skin from 1 chicken breast half and spoon 2 tablespoons of cheese filling under skin. Repeat with remaining breasts and filling. Arrange stuffed breasts, skin side up, in single layer in a broiler pan or shallow roasting pan.

2 Drizzle chicken with the oil and sprinkle with the salt and pepper. Bake 25 to 30 minutes, until skin is golden and juices run clear when chicken is pierced with a fork. Let stand 5 minutes before slicing.

3 To serve, cut each chicken breast into ½-inch slices. Arrange the lettuce on each of 8 dinner plates, then top with 1 cup Black Bean Salad, sliced chicken, and 3 tablespoons dressing. Makes 8 servings.

Black Bean Salad: Combine the black beans, tomatoes, avocados, green onions, lime juice, vegetable oil, cumin, salt, and pepper in a medium bowl. Toss to coat well. Makes 8 cups.

Creamy Cilantro Dressing: Combine the cilantro, sour cream, mayonnaise, lime juice, and garlic in a blender; blend until smooth. Stir in the lime peel, and salt and pepper to taste. Cover and refrigerate until ready to use. Makes 1½ cups.

PER SERVING		DAILY GOAL
Calories	800	2,000 (F), 2,500 (M)
Total Fat	54 g	60 g or less (F), 70 g or less (M)
Saturated fat	12 g	20 g or less (F), 23 g or less (M)
Cholesterol	166 mg	300 mg or less
Sodium	738 mg	2,400 mg or less
Carbohydrates	24 g	250 g or more
Protein	55 g	55 g to 90 g

HOT 'N' HEALTHY CHICKEN ENCHILADAS

Tortillas are usually dipped in oil to soften them for enchiladas. Our lighter version skips this step, and uses low-fat cheese and sour cream.

Ⓜ *Microwave*
▼ *Low-fat*
   Prep time: 10 minutes
   Cooking time: 45 minutes plus standing
Ⓞ *Degree of difficulty: easy*

   4 **cups water**
   1 **teaspoon salt**
   1 **teaspoon black peppercorns**
   ¼ **bay leaf**
   1 **pound boneless, skinless chicken breasts**
   2 **cups Spicy Tomato Sauce, divided (recipe at right)**
   1 **cup shredded low-fat cheddar cheese, divided**
   4 **large (10-inch) flour tortillas**
   ⅓ **cup low-fat sour cream**
      Sliced green onions

1 Combine the water, salt, peppercorns, bay leaf, and chicken in a large skillet. Bring to a boil. Reduce heat and simmer until chicken is firm to the touch, for 8 to 10 minutes. Remove chicken from liquid and shred coarsely.

2 Spread ½ cup of Spicy Tomato Sauce in the bottom of a 10-inch microwave-proof dish. Toss chicken in a bowl with ½ cup more of the sauce. Sprinkle 1 generous tablespoon of cheese and about ½ cup of the shredded chicken mixture down the center of each tortilla. Roll up and place seam side down in the prepared dish.

3 Spread the tops of tortillas evenly with remaining sauce and sprinkle with remaining cheese. Cover with wax paper or glass lid. Microwave on medium-high (70% power) for 8 to 9 minutes, turning dish once. Dollop tops with sour cream and sprinkle with green onions. Makes 4 servings.

PER SERVING		DAILY GOAL	
Calories	540	2,000 (F), 2,500 (M)	
Total Fat	16 g	60 g or less (F), 70 g or less (M)	
Saturated fat	5.5 g	20 g or less (F), 23 g or less (M)	
Cholesterol	92 mg	300 mg or less	
Sodium	1,781 mg	2,400 mg or less	
Carbohydrates	53 g	250 g or more	
Protein	44 g	55 g to 90 g	

SPICY TOMATO SAUCE

This all purpose tomato sauce can give any meal a Southwestern flavor by spooning it over steamed vegetables.

▼ *Low-fat*
▽ *Low-calorie*
   Prep time: 10 minutes
   Cooking time: 25 minutes
Ⓞ *Degree of difficulty: easy*

   2 **tablespoons vegetable oil**
   2 **cups chopped onions**
   1 **tablespoon minced jalapeño chilies**
   1 **tablespoon minced garlic**
   2 **teaspoons chili powder**
   1 **teaspoon cumin**
   ½ **teaspoon salt**
   1 **can (35 ounces) plum tomatoes**

1 Heat the vegetable oil in a large saucepan over medium heat. Add the onions; cover and cook, stirring occasionally, until translucent, for 5 minutes. Stir in the jalapeño pepper and garlic; cook for 30 seconds. Add the chili powder, cumin, and salt; cook for 30 seconds more.

2 Stir in the tomatoes, breaking up pieces with a spoon. Increase heat to high and bring to a boil. Reduce heat to medium-high and cook sauce partially covered for 20 minutes.

3 Transfer 3 cups of the sauce to a food processor or blender, and puree. Return to saucepan to combine. Makes 4 cups.

PER 1/2 CUP SERVING		DAILY GOAL
Calories	55	2,000 (F), 2,500 (M)
Total Fat	2 g	60 g or less (F), 70 g or less (M)
Saturated fat	.2 g	20 g or less (F), 23 g or less (M)
Cholesterol	0 mg	300 mg or less
Sodium	347 mg	2,400 mg or less
Carbohydrates	10 g	250 g or more
Protein	2 g	55 g to 90 g

ARROZ CON POLLO

Our adaptation of this classic uses black beans, the caviar of the Southwest.

Prep time: 20 minutes
Cooking time: 25 minutes
○ *Degree of difficulty: easy*

1 **tablespoon vegetable oil**
1 **chicken (3 to 3½ pounds), cut up**
1 **cup chopped onions**
1 **tablespoon minced garlic**
2 **teaspoons cumin**
1 **cup long-grain rice**
1 **can (13¾ *or* 14½ ounces) chicken broth plus enough water to equal 2 cups liquid**
1 **can (4 ounces) chopped green chilies, with liquid**
½ **teaspoon salt**
½ **teaspoon freshly ground pepper**
1 **can (15 ounces) black beans, drained and rinsed**
1 **can (14 ounces) plum tomatoes, drained and chopped**
⅓ **cup chopped fresh cilantro**
   Lime wedges, for garnish

1 Heat the oil in a large deep skillet or Dutch oven over medium-high heat. Rinse the chicken and pat dry.

2 Add half the chicken to skillet and brown well, about 5 minutes per side. Transfer to a plate. Repeat with remaining chicken.

3 Add the onions to skillet and cook, stirring, until browned. Add the garlic, cumin, and rice; cook, stirring, for 1 minute. Stir in the chicken broth and water, green chilies, salt, and pepper. Bring to a boil.

4 Return chicken to skillet. Cover and simmer over medium heat until rice is tender, about 20 minutes. Stir in the beans and tomatoes. Cover and simmer for 5 minutes more. Stir in the cilantro. Serve with lime wedges. Makes 6 servings.

PER SERVING		DAILY GOAL
Calories	575	2,000 (F), 2,500 (M)
Total Fat	29 g	60 g or less (F), 70 g or less (M)
Saturated fat	7.5 g	20 g or less (F), 23 g or less (M)
Cholesterol	125 mg	300 mg or less
Sodium	982 mg	2,400 mg or less
Carbohydrates	39 g	250 g or more
Protein	38 g	55 g to 90 g

CHICKEN AND TORTILLA SOUP

This quick and comforting soup is a wonderful way to use leftover cooked chicken and tortillas. If available, try whole wheat or blue corn tortillas for a toasted, nutty flavor.

▽ *Low-calorie*
Prep time: 20 minutes
Cooking time: 20 minutes
○ *Degree of difficulty: easy*

2 **tablespoons vegetable oil**
4 **corn tortillas, halved and jullienned**
1 **cup chopped onions**
2 **teaspoons minced garlic**
½ **to 1 jalapeño chili, seeded and chopped**
4 **cans (13¾ *or* 14½ ounces each) chicken broth**
2 **cups chopped cooked chicken**
1 **cup whole-kernel corn**
½ **cup chopped red pepper**
¼ **cup chopped fresh cilantro**
1 **tablespoon fresh lime juice**
2 **teaspoons cumin**

1 Heat the oil in a Dutch oven over medium-high heat. Add the tortilla strips and cook until crisp, for 2 to 3 minutes. Remove with a slotted spoon; drain on paper towels.

2 Add the onions, garlic, and jalapeño to Dutch oven; cook for 3 minutes. Add the chicken broth, chicken, corn, red pepper, cilantro, lime juice, and cumin; simmer for 10 minutes. Spoon into bowls and top each with tortilla strips. Makes 6 servings.

PER SERVING		DAILY GOAL
Calories	245	2,000 (F), 2,500 (M)
Total Fat	12 g	60 g or less (F), 70 g or less (M)
Saturated fat	2 g	20 g or less (F), 23 g or less (M)
Cholesterol	42 mg	300 mg or less
Sodium	1438 mg	2,400 mg or less
Carbohydrates	18 g	250 g or more
Protein	18 g	55 g to 90 g

SKILLET CHICKEN OLÉ

If you need dinner in a flash, this recipe goes from stovetop to table in less than 20 minutes. Use your favorite enchilada sauce, mild or hot.

▽ *Low-calorie*
Prep time: 5 minutes
Cooking time: 7 to 10 minutes
○ *Degree of difficulty: easy*

1 **tablespoon vegetable oil**
1 **pound chicken cutlets, about ½ inch thick**
Salt
Freshly ground pepper
¼ **cup prepared enchilada sauce**
1 **can (4 ounces) whole green chilies, drained and cut into thick strips**
4 **ounces sliced Monterey jack cheese**
2 **tablespoons chopped fresh cilantro**
Sour cream
Warm tortillas

1 Heat the oil in a large skillet over medium-high heat. Sprinkle both sides of the chicken cutlets with salt and pepper. Add cutlets to skillet and sauté until golden brown, for 2 to 2½ minutes per side. Reduce heat to medium.

2 Spoon the enchilada sauce over chicken; top with the chilies and Monterey jack cheese. Cover skillet and cook until cheese melts, about 3 minutes.

3 Transfer chicken to a serving platter and sprinkle with cilantro. Serve with sour cream and tortillas. Makes 4 servings.

PER SERVING		DAILY GOAL
Calories	275	2,000 (F), 2,500 (M)
Total Fat	13 g	60 g or less (F), 70 g or less (M)
Saturated fat	1 g	20 g or less (F), 23 g or less (M)
Cholesterol	91 mg	300 mg or less
Sodium	535 mg	2,400 mg or less
Carbohydrates	3 g	250 g or more
Protein	34 g	55 g to 90 g

MEXICAN CHICKEN LIME STEW

Here's a do-ahead stew that features a wonderful homemade chicken broth spiked with red and green chilies.

▼ *Low-fat*
▽ *Low-calorie*
   Prep time: 1¼ hours plus chilling
   Cooking time: 25 minutes
○ *Degree of difficulty: easy*

1   chicken (3 pounds), cut up
1   can (13¾ or 14½ ounces) chicken
      broth
6   cups water
1   cup chopped onions
3   whole garlic cloves
1   teaspoon salt, divided
½   teaspoon red pepper flakes
1   can (14 ounces) whole tomatoes,
      chopped
½   cup minced onion
¼   cup chopped green chilies
¼   teaspoon chili powder
1   lime, halved, plus squeezed juice
1   package (10 ounces) frozen whole-
      kernel corn
1   cup cooked rice

Lime slices, for garnish
¼   cup chopped fresh cilantro, for
      garnish

1 Combine the chicken, chicken broth, water, onions, garlic, ½ teaspoon of the salt, and red pepper flakes in a Dutch oven. Bring just to a boil. Reduce heat and simmer gently for 45 minutes.

2 Drain, reserving broth and chicken separately. Remove meat from bones and dice; cover and refrigerate. Freeze soup for 1 hour or refrigerate overnight; skim fat.

3 Combine the chicken broth, tomatoes, onion, green chilies, remaining ½ teaspoon salt, and chili powder in a Dutch oven. Bring to a boil. Reduce heat and simmer 10 minutes.

4 Add the lime halves and juice, corn, rice, and chicken to Dutch oven. Simmer for 5 minutes. Remove lime. Garnish with lime slices and cilantro. Makes 10 cups.

PER SERVING		DAILY GOAL
Calories	155	2,000 (F), 2,500 (M)
Total Fat	3 g	60 g or less (F), 70 g or less (M)
Saturated fat	1 g	20 g or less (F), 23 g or less (M)
Cholesterol	46 mg	300 mg or less
Sodium	542 mg	2,400 mg or less
Carbohydrates	17 g	250 g or more
Protein	16 g	55 g to 90

CHICKEN TAMALES

Homemade tamales are comfort food, Southwestern style. Corn husks are traditionally used for steaming tamales, but foil is a convenient alternative. Ground turkey can also be substituted for the chicken.

Prep time: 40 minutes plus soaking
Cooking time: 40 minutes
Degree of difficulty: moderate

½ **cup chopped onion**
1½ **teaspoons minced garlic**
½ **teaspoon cumin**
¾ **teaspoon salt, divided**
  Freshly ground pepper
½ **pound ground chicken**
2 **tablespoons canned chopped green chilies**
¾ **cup chicken broth**
¼ **cup water**
¼ **cup vegetable oil**
1 **cup yellow cornmeal**
½ **teaspoon baking powder**
  Pinch ground red pepper
1 **cup whole-kernel corn**
¼ **cup chopped green onions**

½ **package dried corn husks for tamales (about 20), soaked for 2 hours***
  Prepared salsa, for garnish

1 For filling, spray a medium nonstick skillet with vegetable cooking spray; heat over medium heat. Add the onion and cook until translucent, about 3 minutes. Stir in the garlic, cumin, ¼ teaspoon of the salt, and pinch of pepper; cook for 30 seconds. Add the ground chicken, stirring with a spoon to break the meat up. Cook until meat is opaque, about 5 minutes. Stir in the green chilies. Cool for 10 minutes.

2 Meanwhile, bring the chicken broth, water, and oil to a boil in a small saucepan. Combine the cornmeal, baking powder, red pepper, ¼ teaspoon freshly ground pepper, and remaining ½ teaspoon salt, in a food processor. With the machine on, pour hot broth mixture through the feed tube in a steady stream and process until smooth. Transfer to a medium bowl and stir in the corn and green onions.

3 Select 2 equal-size husks and overlap long edges. Spoon a scant ⅓ cup cornmeal mixture down the center; spread lightly. Spoon 3 tablespoons of filling on top of cornmeal.

4 Roll one long edge of husk inward, cigar-fashion, to enclose filling. Tie each end with a string or thin strip of husk. Repeat with remaining husks, cornmeal mixture, and filling to make a total of 8 tamales.

5 Arrange tamales in a single layer on a steamer rack over boiling water in large pot or skillet. Cover and steam for 40 minutes, adding more boiling water as needed. Serve with salsa. Makes 4 servings.

*Note: Dried corn husks are available at Latin-American specialty markets. Or cut eight 8x6-inch sheets of aluminum foil and fill as directed. Fold foil, enclosing filling in cornmeal mixture, and crimp edges securely. Steam as directed above.

PER SERVING		DAILY GOAL
Calories	195	2,000 (F), 2,500 (M)
Total Fat	10 g	60 g or less (F), 70 g or less (M)
Saturated fat	2 g	20 g or less (F), 23 g or less (M)
Cholesterol	23 mg	300 mg or less
Sodium	384 mg	2,400 mg or less
Carbohydrates	18 g	250 g or more
Protein	8 g	55 g to 90 g

ROASTED CHICKEN WITH CILANTRO

Broiling the chicken during the last 5 minutes of cooking gives the skin a wonderful golden color and an extra crispy texture. You can also try this recipe with cornish game hens.

Prep time: 10 minutes
Cooking time: 45 minutes plus
*   standing*
○ *Degree of difficulty: easy*

2   **tablespoons chopped fresh cilantro**
2   **garlic cloves, minced**
2   **small chickens (2 to 2½ pounds each), halved**
1   **teaspoon salt**
½   **teaspoon red pepper flakes**
1   **large lemon, sliced thin**
    Cilantro sprigs, for garnish

1 Place the oven rack in center position. Preheat oven to 425°F. Combine the cilantro and garlic in a bowl. Loosen the skin from the chicken halves. Spoon the cilantro-garlic mixture under the skin of each chicken half. Sprinkle chicken with salt and red pepper flakes. Arrange halves, skin side up, on broiler pan. Top with lemon slices.

2 Roast chicken 40 minutes or until juices run clear when chicken is pierced with a fork. Increase heat to broil. Broil chicken 4 inches from heat source for 5 minutes. Transfer to a serving platter. Garnish with cilantro sprigs and serve with pan drippings. Makes 4 servings.

PER SERVING		DAILY GOAL	
Calories	545	2,000 (F), 2,500 (M)	
Total Fat	31 g	60 g or less (F), 70 g or less (M)	
Saturated fat	9 g	20 g or less (F), 23 g or less (M)	
Cholesterol	198 mg	300 mg or less	
Sodium	736 mg	2,400 mg or less	
Carbohydrates	4 g	250 g or more	
Protein	62 g	55 g to 90 g	

TEX-MEX CHICKEN

To crisp up this flavorful bird, preheat the broiler. Then, transfer the chicken to a roasting pan and place it on the lowest oven rack. Broil until skin is golden, about 2 minutes.

Ⓜ *Microwave*
   Prep time: 10 minutes plus marinating
   Microwave time: 1 hour 10 minutes
Ⓞ *Degree of difficulty: easy*

½ **cup orange juice**
2 **tablespoons white wine vinegar**
2 **teaspoons minced garlic**
1½ **teaspoons cumin**
1 **teaspoon oregano**
½ **teaspoon salt**
¼ **teaspoon freshly ground pepper**
1 **roasting chicken (7 pounds)**

1 For marinade, combine the orange juice, wine vinegar, garlic, cumin, oregano, salt, and pepper in a glass bowl. Rinse chicken and pat dry. Remove the giblets and excess fat from body cavity. Rub marinade inside and out. Place chicken with marinade in a large plastic storage bag and seal. Refrigerate up to 24 hours, turning bag once.

2 Remove chicken from bag. Tie the legs together with string and tuck wings under. Pour the remaining marinade into cavity and place chicken breast-side down in a microwave proof dish. Cover with wax paper, tucking ends in around chicken.

3 Microwave on high (100% power) for 5 minutes. Then microwave on medium (50% power) for 35 minutes. Turn over, cover, and microwave on medium (50% power) about 30 minutes more or until a meat thermometer inserted in the thickest part of the thigh reaches 180°F. Let stand covered for 15 minutes. Makes 8 servings.

PER SERVING		DAILY GOAL
Calories	470	2,000 (F), 2,500 (M)
Total Fat	28 g	60 g or less (F), 70 g or less (M)
Saturated fat	8g	20 g or less (F), 23 g or less (M)
Cholesterol	156 mg	300 mg or less
Sodium	287 mg	2,400 mg or less
Carbohydrates	2 g	250 g or more
Protein	49 g	55 g to 90 g

TEXAS HEAT-WAVE CHICKEN WINGS

You'll wow the crowd when you serve these as an appetizer. They're also great as the main event. Our trio of sauces are for those who like it hot, hotter, and hottest!

Prep time: 20 minutes
Cooking time: 50 minutes
○ *Degree of difficulty: easy*

1 **cup cider vinegar**
½ **cup water**
1 **cup minced onions**
2 **teaspoons sugar**
2 **teaspoons red pepper flakes**
1 **teaspoon salt**
1 **teaspoon freshly ground pepper**
6 **pounds chicken wings, tips**
   trimmed
   Hot, Hotter, *or* Hottest Sauce
   (recipes at right)

1 Preheat oven to 425°F. Adjust 2 oven racks to center and lowest oven positions. Line 2 jelly-roll pans or roasting pans with foil. Set aside.

2 Combine the vinegar, water, onions, sugar, red pepper flakes, salt, and pepper in a small saucepan. Bring to a boil. Reduce heat and simmer 5 minutes.

3 Place the chicken wings in the prepared pans and brush ½ cup of the vinegar sauce over wings in each pan. Bake for 20 minutes. Turn wings over and brush remaining sauce on top. Switch positions of pans. Bake for 20 minutes more. Turn wings over and switch pans again; bake for 10 minutes more. Serve with your choice of sauces. Makes 6 main-dish servings.

PER SERVING WITHOUT HOD SAUCE		DAILY GOAL
Calories	510	2,000 (F), 2,500 (M)
Total Fat	33 g	60 g or less (F), 70 g or less (M)
Saturated fat	9 g	20 g or less (F), 23 g or less (M)
Cholesterol	144 mg	300 mg or less
Sodium	324 mg	2,400 mg or less
Carbohydrates	3 g	250 g or more
Protein	46 g	55 g to 90 g

Hot Sauce: Combine ¼ cup Dijon mustard, ¼ cup sour cream, ¼ cup mayonnaise, and ½ teaspoon red pepper sauce in a small bowl. (Can be made ahead. Cover and refrigerate up to 24 hours.) Makes ¾ cup.

PER TABLESPOON		DAILY GOAL
Calories	50	2,000 (F), 2,500 (M)
Total Fat	5 g	60 g or less (F), 70 g or less (M)
Saturated fat	1 g	20 g or less (F), 23 g or less (M)
Cholesterol	5 mg	300 mg or less
Sodium	184 mg	2,400 mg or less
Carbohydrates	1 g	250 g or more
Protein	0 g	55 g to 90 g

Hotter Sauce: Combine ½ cup ketchup, 2 tablespoons firmly packed brown sugar, and 2 teaspoons red pepper flakes in a 1-cup microwave proof measure. Microwave on high (100% power) 1 to 1½ minutes, until boiling. Cool. (Can be made ahead. Cover and refrigerate up to 24 hours.) Makes ⅔ cup.

PER TABLESPOON		DAILY GOAL
Calories	25	2,000 (F), 2,500 (M)
Total Fat	0 g	60 g or less (F), 70 g or less (M)
Saturated fat	0 g	20 g or less (F), 23 g or less (M)
Cholesterol	0 mg	300 mg or less
Sodium	143 mg	2,400 mg or less
Carbohydrates	6 g	250 g or more
Protein	0 g	55 g to 90 g

Hottest Sauce: Combine ¼ cup red pepper sauce, ¼ cup prepared horseradish, ¼ cup minced onion, and ¼ cup minced green pepper in a bowl. (Can be made ahead. Cover and refrigerate up to 4 hours.) Makes ¾ cup.

PER TABLESPOON		DAILY GOAL
Calories	5	2,000 (F), 2,500 (M)
Total Fat	0 g	60 g or less (F), 70 g or less (M)
Saturated fat	0 g	20 g or less (F), 23 g or less (M)
Cholesterol	0 mg	300 mg or less
Sodium	136 mg	2,400 mg or less
Carbohydrates	1 g	250 g or more
Protein	0 g	55 g to 90 g

SANTA FE CHICKEN CLUB SANDWICH

Searing the chicken cutlets in a cast iron skillet gives this sandwich a wonderful smoky flavor without turning on an outdoor grill.

Prep time: 30 minutes plus marinating
Cooking time: 20 minutes
Degree of difficulty: easy

- 4 **chicken cutlets (about 1 pound), about ½ inch thick**
- ¼ **cup plus 1 tablespoon fresh lime juice, divided**
- 4 **tablespoons chopped fresh cilantro, divided**
- 4 **tablespoons diced onion, divided**
- 3 **teaspoons minced jalapeño chilies, divided**
  Salt
  Freshly ground pepper
- 1 **tablespoon olive oil**
- 4 **soft rolls**
  Lettuce
- 1 **tomato, sliced**
- 1 **avocado, sliced**

1 Arrange the chicken in a single layer in a large glass baking dish. Combine ¼ cup of the lime juice, 2 tablespoons of the cilantro, 2 tablespoons of the onion and 1½ teaspoons of the jalapeño chilies in a small cup. Pour over chicken, turning to coat. Cover and refrigerate for 1 hour, turning once.

2 Rinse chicken and pat dry. Season both sides with salt and pepper. Lightly oil a large cast-iron skillet; heat over medium-high heat. Add half the chicken and cook until golden brown, about 2 minutes per side. Keep warm in oven. Repeat with remaining chicken.

3 For dressing, combine 1 tablespoon olive oil with the remaining 1 tablepoon lime juice, remaining cilantro, onions, and jalapeño chilies and ¼ teaspoon salt in a small bowl.

4 Slice each roll in half crosswise. On the bottom of each roll layer a lettuce leaf, a chicken cutlet, and equal amounts of avocado and tomato slices. Sprinkle the tomato slices lightly with additional salt and pepper, if desired. Drizzle the dressing over each. Replace tops of rolls. Makes 4 sandwiches.

PER SERVING		DAILY GOAL
Calories	350	2,000 (F), 2,500 (M)
Total Fat	16 g	60 g or less (F), 70 g or less (M)
Saturated fat	3 g	20 g or less (F), 23 g or less (M)
Cholesterol	66 mg	300 mg or less
Sodium	367 mg	2,400 mg or less
Carbohydrates	21 g	250 g or more
Protein	30 g	55 g to 90 g

NOTES

SOUTHWEST CHICKEN BURGERS

Read the label carefully to look for chicken breast meat that contains about 97% lean meat. These burgers can also be prepared with ground turkey.

▽ *Low-calorie*
Prep time: 15 minutes
Cooking time: 10 minutes
○ *Degree of difficulty: easy*

1 **pound ground chicken**
½ **cup shredded zucchini**
2 **tablespoons canned chopped green chilies**
½ **teaspoon cumin**
½ **teaspoon salt**
½ **teaspoon freshly ground pepper**
½ **cup prepared salsa**
2 **tablespoons chopped green onions**
2 **tablespoons chopped fresh cilantro**
1 **tablespoon plain nonfat yogurt**
4 **hamburger rolls, split and toasted**
 Lettuce leaves

1 Combine the chicken, zucchini, green chilies, cumin, salt, and pepper in a bowl. Shape into four ½-inch-thick patties.

2 Coat a large non-stick skillet with vegetable cooking spray and heat over medium-high heat. Add the patties and cook for 5 minutes per side.

3 Combine salsa, green onions, cilantro, and yogurt in a small bowl. Place each burger on the bottom half of a roll. Top each with 3 tablespoons of the salsa mixture, lettuce, and the top half of the roll. Makes 4 servings.

PER SERVING		DAILY GOAL	
Calories	315	2,000 (F), 2,500 (M)	
Total Fat	13 g	60 g or less (F), 70 g or less (M)	
Saturated fat	3 g	20 g or less (F), 23 g or less (M)	
Cholesterol	97 mg	300 mg or less	
Sodium	778 mg	2,400 mg or less	
Carbohydrates	25 g	250 g or more	
Protein	24 g	55 g to 90 g	

NOTES

79

CHICKEN GOOD

AND QUICK

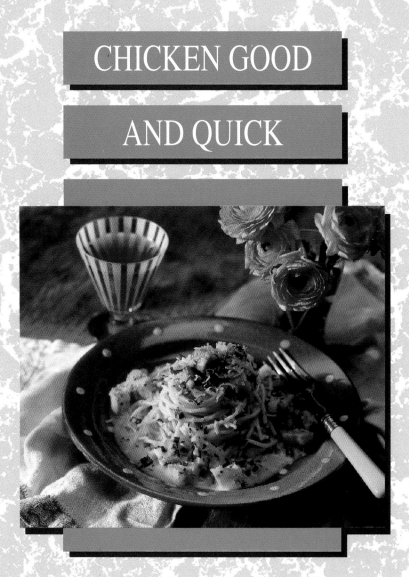

When it's dinnertime in the fast lane, chicken takes the lead. Here's a selection of fabulous recipes that are long on flavor and perfect for any occasion when you're short on time. You'll love our Crispy Roast Herb Chicken with Polenta that's ready—start to finish—in less than 30 minutes. Or choose Spicy Chicken Alfredo on thin spaghetti or a Warm Chicken and Pesto Vegetable Sandwich on dark bread. Each one is a quick, tasty meal without a lot of bother.

CHICKEN PARMESAN PRONTO

Use your favorite marinara sauce for this easy-on-the cook dish. This dish is perfect served with angel-hair pasta.

Prep time: 20 minutes
Baking time: 10 minutes
Degree of difficulty: easy

- 4 **boneless, skinless chicken breast halves (about 1 pound)**
- ¼ **teaspoon salt**
- ¼ **teaspoon freshly ground pepper**
- ¼ **cup all-purpose flour**
- 1 **large egg, beaten**
- ½ **cup plain dry bread crumbs**
- 2 **tablespoons olive oil**
- 1 **cup sliced fresh mushrooms**
- 1 **jar (14 *or* 14½ ounces) pizza-style sauce *or* chunky marinara sauce**
- 1 **tablespoon chopped fresh parsley**
- 1 **medium zucchini, cut lengthwise into 8 slices**
- 1 **cup shredded mozzarella cheese**

1 Preheat oven to 375°F. Place the chicken between 2 sheets of wax paper. Pound to ½ inch thick with a rolling pin or mallet. Sprinkle chicken with salt and pepper.

2 Place the flour, beaten egg, and bread crumbs in 3 separate, shallow dishes. Dip chicken in flour, shaking off any excess, then in egg, then in crumbs, pressing firmly to coat.

3 Heat the oil in a skillet over medium-high heat. Cook chicken until golden, about 3 to 4 minutes per side. Transfer chicken to a 13x9-inch shallow baking dish. Add the mushrooms to skillet; cook for 30 seconds. Add the sauce and parsley; cook, stirring, for 3 minutes.

4 Layer the zucchini in a shallow microwave-proof dish. Sprinkle it with 1 tablespoon water. Cover with wax paper or a paper towel. Microwave on high (100% power) for 2 minutes; drain.

5 Place 2 zucchini slices in an X pattern on each chicken breast. Pour sauce evenly over zucchini and sprinkle with the cheese. Bake uncovered about 10 minutes or until cheese is melted. Makes 4 servings.

PER SERVING		DAILY GOAL
Calories	425	2,000 (F), 2,500 (M)
Total Fat	19 g	60 g or less (F), 70 g or less (M)
Saturated fat	6 g	20 g or less (F), 23 g or less (M)
Cholesterol	142 mg	300 mg or less
Sodium	847 mg	2,400 mg or less
Carbohydrates	20 g	250 g or more
Protein	39 g	55 g to 90 g

NOTES

CHEAT-THE-CLOCK CASSOULET

It's hard to believe that you can get such great flavor from this cassoulet when the traditional French stew simmers for hours.

Prep time: 25 minutes
Cooking time: 35 minutes
○ *Degree of difficulty: easy*

3 slices bacon, diced
6 chicken thighs (2 pounds)
½ teaspoon salt
¼ teaspoon freshly ground pepper
1 cup chopped onions
2½ teaspoons minced garlic, divided
½ cup white wine
1 can (14 ounces) tomatoes, drained
½ bay leaf
¼ teaspoon thyme
¼ teaspoon rosemary
2 cans (19 ounces each) cannellini
    beans, drained and rinsed
8 ounces light kielbasa sausage, cut
    into ½-inch chunks
½ cup fresh bread crumbs
¼ cup chopped fresh parsley

1 Cook the bacon in a large skillet over medium-high heat until crisp; drain on paper towels. Discard all but 1 tablespoon of drippings from skillet.

2 Sprinkle the chicken with salt and pepper. Add chicken to skillet and brown on both sides, about 5 minutes. Remove chicken from pan and set aside. Add the onions to skillet and cook over medium heat until tender, about 5 minutes. Add 2 teaspoons of the garlic and cook 30 seconds. Carefully add the wine, tomatoes, bay leaf, thyme, and rosemary, stirring to break up tomatoes.

3 Return chicken to skillet and bring just to a boil. Reduce heat and simmer covered for 20 minutes. Add the beans and sausage; simmer uncovered for 10 minutes more.

4 Meanwhile, preheat broiler. Combine the bread crumbs, parsley, and the remaining ½ teaspoon garlic in a small bowl. Remove bay leaf from cassoulet and stir in bacon. Spoon into a shallow 2-quart baking dish and sprinkle evenly with crumbs. Broil 1 minute or until golden. Makes 6 servings.

PER SERVING		DAILY GOAL
Calories	545	2,000 (F), 2,500 (M)
Total Fat	31 g	60 g or less (F), 70 g or less (M)
Saturated fat	6 g	20 g or less (F), 23 g or less (M)
Cholesterol	131 mg	300 mg or less
Sodium	994 mg	2,400 mg or less
Carbohydrates	28 g	250 g or more
Protein	38 g	55 g to 90 g

NOTES

_____
_____
_____
_____
_____
_____
_____
_____
_____
_____
_____
_____
_____

SPICY CHICKEN ALFREDO

Go ahead and indulge! The richness of this cream sauce with tender morsels of chicken and freshly grated Parmesan cheese helps soothe the fiery spices in this luxurious pasta entrée. *Also pictured on page 80.*

Prep time: 15 minutes
Cooking time: 7 minutes
O *Degree of difficulty: easy*

 2 **tablespoons butter *or* margarine**
 1 **teaspoon minced garlic**
12 **ounces boneless, skinless chicken breasts, cubed**
 1 **teaspoon salt**
 ½ **teaspoon thyme**
 ¼ **teaspoon onion powder**
 ¼ **teaspoon rubbed sage**
 ¼ **teaspoon freshly ground pepper**
 ¼ **teaspoon white pepper**
  Pinch ground red pepper
 ⅓ **cup chopped green onions**
 1 **cup heavy *or* whipping cream**
12 **ounces thin spaghetti, cooked according to package directions**

 2 **tablespoons chopped fresh parsley**
  Freshly grated Parmesan cheese

1 Melt the butter in a large skillet over medium-high heat. Add the garlic and cook for 30 seconds. Stir in the chicken and seasonings; cook until lightly browned, about 3 minutes. Stir in the green onions; cook for 1 minute more. Carefully add the cream. Increase heat to high and boil until slightly thickened, about 2 minutes.

2 Combine the chicken mixture, pasta, and parsley in a serving bowl; toss to mix. Pass Parmesan cheese. Makes 4 servings.

PER SERVING		DAILY GOAL
Calories	670	2,000 (F), 2,500 (M)
Total Fat	30 g	60 g or less (F), 70 g or less (M)
Saturated fat	17 g	20 g or less (F), 23 g or less (M)
Cholesterol	146 mg	300 mg or less
Sodium	695 mg	2,400 mg or less
Carbohydrates	66 g	250 g or more
Protein	32 g	55 g to 90 g

CHICKEN MADEIRA WITH PROSCIUTTO

Madeira, a wine produced in Portugal, has a fruity, sweet taste which is a perfect complement to chicken.

Prep time: 5 minutes
Cooking time: 20 minutes
○ *Degree of difficulty: easy*

2 **tablespoons butter, divided (no substitutions)**
1 **tablespoon olive oil**
8 **boneless chicken thighs with skin, (1½ pounds)**
  Salt
  Freshly ground pepper
¼ **cup chopped shallots**
¼ **pound small fresh mushroom caps**
¼ **cup diced prosciutto ham**
⅓ **cup Madeira wine**
½ **cup chicken broth**
1 **tablespoon chopped fresh parsley**

1 Heat 1 tablespoon of the butter and the olive oil in a large skillet over medium-high heat just until butter stops foaming. Season the chicken with salt and pepper. Add thighs to skillet and cook until golden brown, 7 minutes per side. Transfer to a platter; cover and keep warm.

2 Drain all but 1 tablespoon of the drippings from skillet. Add the shallots, mushrooms, and prosciutto; cook, stirring, 2 minutes. Add the Madeira, stirring to scrape up any browned bits. Add the chicken broth; bring to a boil.

3 Return chicken to skillet; cook over high heat 3 minutes or until the sauce is reduced by half. Transfer chicken to a heated serving platter. Stir the parsley into sauce. Remove skillet from heat and whisk in the remaining 1 tablespoon of butter. Spoon sauce over chicken. Makes 4 servings.

PER SERVING		DAILY GOAL	
Calories	430	2,000 (F), 2,500 (M)	
Total Fat	28 g	60 g or less (F), 70 g or less (M)	
Saturated fat	9 g	20 g or less (F), 23 g or less (M)	
Cholesterol	127 mg	300 mg or less	
Sodium	466 mg	2,400 mg or less	
Carbohydrates	5 g	250 g or more	
Protein	31 g	55 g to 90 g	

ROAST HERB CHICKEN WITH POLENTA

We found the key to successfully roasting a whole chicken in the microwave: Use a covered casserole to guarantee moistness; then just pop the bird under the broiler to brown and crisp the skin.

Ⓜ *Microwave*
▽ *Low-calorie*
  Prep time: 15 minutes
  Cooking time: 25 minutes
○ *Degree of difficulty: easy*

1 **small whole chicken (2½ pounds)**
½ **lemon, cut into 2 wedges**
2 **garlic cloves, smashed**
4 **fresh parsley sprigs**
¼ **teaspoon salt**
¼ **teaspoon freshly ground pepper**
¼ **teaspoon thyme**
  Polenta with Parmesan and Walnuts (recipe at right)

1 Remove the giblets from chicken cavity. Rinse the chicken and pat it dry. Stuff cavity with the lemon and garlic cloves. Tuck wings under. Place the parsley under skin. Sprinkle chicken with the salt, pepper, and thyme. Tie legs together with kitchen string.

2 Place chicken, breast side down, on a microwave-proof roasting rack in a 5-quart microwave-proof casserole with lid. Cover and microwave on high (100% power) for 5 minutes. Turn chicken breast side up and microwave covered for 6 minutes. Rotate dish halfway and microwave about 6 minutes more or until meat thermometer inserted into thickest part of the thigh reaches 180°F. Let stand covered for 5 minutes.

3 Adjust the broiler pan to lowest position. Preheat broiler. Place chicken in a roasting pan; broil until skin is golden, 2 minutes. Serve with Polenta with Parmesan and Walnuts. Makes 4 servings.

PER SERVING		DAILY GOAL
Calories	305	2,000 (F), 2,500 (M)
Total Fat	17 g	60 g or less (F), 70 g or less (M)
Saturated fat	4 g	20 g or less (F), 23 g or less (M)
Cholesterol	110 mg	300 mg or less
Sodium	239 mg	2,400 mg or less
Carbohydrates	2 g	250 g or more
Protein	34 g	55 g to 90 g

POLENTA WITH PARMESAN AND WALNUTS

▽ *Low-calorie*
Prep time: 5 minutes
Cooking time: 20 minutes
○ *Degree of difficulty: easy*

4 **cups water**
1 **cup yellow cornmeal**
¾ **teaspoon salt**
⅔ **cup freshly grated Parmesan cheese**
2 **tablespoons butter** *or* **margarine**
¼ **teaspoon freshly ground pepper**
¼ **cup toasted, chopped walnuts**

1 Bring the water to a boil in a large saucepan. Reduce heat to low and gradually whisk in the cornmeal and salt. Cook, stirring occasionally, 15 minutes.

2 Stir in the Parmesan cheese, butter or margarine, and pepper. Transfer to a serving bowl and sprinkle with the walnuts. Makes 4 servings.

PER SERVING		DAILY GOAL
Calories	300	2,000 (F), 2,500 (M)
Total Fat	16 g	60 g or less (F), 70 g or less (M)
Saturated fat	7 g	20 g or less (F), 23 g or less (M)
Cholesterol	28 mg	300 mg or less
Sodium	777 mg	2,400 mg or less
Carbohydrates	29 g	250 g or more
Protein	11 g	55 g to 90 g

NOTES

_____

_____

_____

_____

_____

_____

_____

_____

_____

_____

_____

SICILIAN GRILLED CHICKEN WITH WATERCRESS

The smoky flavor of the grilled chicken breasts and the peppery tang of the watercress make this speedy entrée a sensational mix of tastes and textures.

▽ *Low-calorie*
   Prep time: 10 minutes
   Cooking time: 8 minutes
○ *Degree of difficulty: easy*

1 **tablespoon fresh lemon juice**
1 **teaspoon anchovy paste**
   Freshly ground pepper
2 **tablespoons olive oil**
1 **tablespoon finely chopped shallots**
4 **boneless, skinless chicken breast halves (1¼ pounds)**
   Salt
4 **cups trimmed watercress**
   Lemon wedges

1 Prepare the grill or preheat the broiler and broiler pan. Whisk the lemon juice with the anchovy paste and ¼ teaspoon pepper in a medium bowl; whisk in the oil and shallots. Set aside.

2 Place the chicken between 2 sheets of wax paper. Pound to ¼ inch thick with rolling pin or mallet. Sprinkle with salt and pepper. Grill over medium coals, or broil 3 inches from heat source, about 4 minutes per side until opaque in center.

3 Meanwhile, toss the watercress with the dressing and arrange on 4 plates. Top with chicken and serve with lemon wedges. Makes 4 servings.

PER SERVING		DAILY GOAL
Calories	225	2,000 (F), 2,500 (M)
Total Fat	9 g	60 g or less (F), 70 g or less (M)
Saturated fat	2 g	20 g or less (F), 23 g or less (M)
Cholesterol	83 mg	300 mg or less
Sodium	161 mg	2,400 mg or less
Carbohydrates	1 g	250 g or more
Protein	34 g	55 g to 90 g

NOTES

SPRING CHICKEN AND ASPARAGUS BUNDLES

Look for pencil-thin asparagus for this colorful microwave entrée.

Ⓜ   *Microwave*
▼   *Low-fat*
▽   *Low-calorie*
    Prep time: 5 minutes
    Cooking time: 8 minutes
O   *Degree of difficulty: easy*

¾   **pound thin asparagus, trimmed to 5 inches**
4   **boneless, skinless chicken breast halves (about 1 pound)**
    Salt
    Freshly ground pepper
2   **teaspoons olive oil, divided**
4   **slices prosciutto ham (about 2 ounces)**
¼   **cup fresh basil leaves**

1 Place the asparagus in a 12x7½x2-inch microwave-proof dish. Cover with plastic wrap or wax paper; vent. Microwave on high (100% power) about 1½ to 2 minutes, just until tender. Transfer to a plate and keep warm.

2 Place the chicken in the same dish, season with salt and pepper, then drizzle with 1 teaspoon of the olive oil. Cover with plastic wrap; vent. Microwave on high (100% power) for 3 to 4 minutes, rearranging chicken halfway through.

3 Cover each prosciutto slice with the basil leaves right side down. Place an equal number of asparagus spears, with tips exposed, at one end of each slice. Starting from one end, roll asparagus in prosciutto.

4 Place the bundles seam side down on top of chicken breasts. Drizzle with the remaining 1 teaspoon olive oil. Cover and microwave on high (100% power) for 1 minute. Let stand for 2 minutes. Baste chicken with juices before serving. Makes 4 servings.

PER SERVING		DAILY GOAL
Calories	195	2,000 (F), 2,500 (M)
Total Fat	6 g	60 g or less (F), 70 g or less (M)
Saturated fat	1 g	20 g or less (F), 23 g or less (M)
Cholesterol	77 mg	300 mg or less
Sodium	338 mg	2,400 mg or less
Carbohydrates	3 g	250 g or more
Protein	33 g	55 g to 90 g

_____
_____
_____
_____
_____
_____
_____
_____
_____
_____
_____
_____
_____
_____

GREEK CHICKEN AND HERBED FETA ROLLS

Your friends and family will be delighted when they bite into one of these cheesy chicken bundles, stuffed with herbs and fresh spinach.

Prep time: 10 minutes
Cooking time: 15 to 20 minutes
Degree of difficulty: moderate

8 **boneless chicken thighs with skin**
    (1½ pounds)
   Salt
   Freshly ground pepper
½ **pound feta cheese, crumbled**
3 **tablespoons chopped fresh parsley**
2 **tablespoons chopped fresh dill**
3 **tablespoons olive oil, divided**
2 **teaspoons lemon juice**
16 **spinach leaves**

1 Preheat oven to 450°F. Season the chicken with salt and pepper. Combine the cheese, parsley, dill, 1 tablespoon of the oil, and lemon juice in a medium bowl. Place chicken skin side down on a work surface. Top each thigh with 2 spinach leaves and 1 heaping tablespoon of the cheese mixture. Fold each thigh in half from the short side and secure with a toothpick.

2 Heat the remaining 2 tablespoons oil in a large skillet over high heat. Add chicken and brown quickly on all sides.

3 Transfer chicken to a rack in a shallow baking pan. Bake for 10 to 15 minutes, or until firm to the touch and juices run clear when chicken is pierced with a fork. Makes 4 servings.

PER SERVING		DAILY GOAL
Calories	400	2,000 (F), 2,500 (M)
Total Fat	32 g	60 g or less (F), 70 g or less (M)
Saturated fat	11 g	20 g or less (F), 23 g or less (M)
Cholesterol	128 mg	300 mg or less
Sodium	517 mg	2,400 mg or less
Carbohydrates	2 g	250 g or more
Protein	25 g	55 g to 90 g

NOTES

91

CHICKEN ADOBO

This Philippine dish couldn't be easier. Simply throw everything into a pot and cook it!

▼ *Low-fat*
Prep time: 10 minutes
Cooking time: 18 minutes
○ *Degree of difficulty: easy*

8 **boneless, skinless chicken thighs (1¼ pounds)**
¼ **cup white vinegar**
¼ **cup soy sauce**
1 **tablespoon vegetable oil**
1 **tablespoon minced garlic**
2 **teaspoons sugar**
½ **bay leaf**
¼ **teaspoon freshly ground pepper**
1 **cup snow peas, trimmed**
1 **cup diced fresh *or* canned pineapple**
1 **cup long-grain rice, cooked**
¼ **cup chopped fresh cilantro**

1 Combine the chicken, vinegar, soy sauce, oil, garlic, sugar, bay leaf, and pepper in a 3-quart saucepan. Bring to a boil, stirring occasionally, over medium-high heat. Reduce heat, cover and simmer, stirring occasionally, for 12 minutes. With a slotted spoon, transfer chicken to a platter; keep warm.

2 Discard bay leaf. Increase heat to high; cook sauce until syrupy, about 5 minutes.

3 Meanwhile, place the snow peas in a microwave-proof dish. Sprinkle with 1 tablespoon water; cover and microwave on high (100% power) for 50 seconds. Drain snow peas and toss with chicken on a serving platter.

4 Arrange the pineapple around chicken on platter; pour the sauce over. Stir the cilantro into the rice and serve on chicken. Makes 4 servings.

PER SERVING		DAILY GOAL
Calories	425	2,000 (F), 2,500 (M)
Total Fat	10 g	60 g or less (F), 70 g or less (M)
Saturated fat	2 g	20 g or less (F), 23 g or less (M)
Cholesterol	118 mg	300 mg or less
Sodium	1,156 mg	2,400 mg or less
Carbohydrates	50 g	250 g or more
Protein	3 g	55 g to 90 g

NOTES

CHICKEN ORIENT EXPRESS

Fresh ginger and tangy orange peel spice up this low-fat chicken and whole-wheat pasta combo.

▼ *Low-fat*
▽ *Low-calorie*
   Prep time: 20 minutes
   Cooking time: 10 minutes
○ *Degree of difficulty: easy*

⅓ **cup fresh orange juice**
¼ **cup reduced-sodium soy sauce**
1 **teaspoon cornstarch**
¼ **teaspoon grated orange peel**
   Pinch freshly ground pepper
¾ **pound boneless, skinless chicken breasts, sliced ½-inch thick**
¼ **cup water**
3 **cups small broccoli pieces**
2 **teaspoons vegetable oil**
1 **teaspoon grated fresh ginger**
   Sesame Wheat Noodles (recipe at right)

1 Combine the orange juice, soy sauce, cornstarch, orange peel, and pepper in a medium glass bowl until smooth. Stir in the chicken; let stand for 10 minutes.

2 Bring the water to a boil in a large non-stick skillet. Add the broccoli, cover and steam for 3 minutes. Drain and reserve.

3 Heat the oil in the same skillet over medium-high heat. Add the ginger; cook for 30 seconds. Add chicken and marinade; cook, stirring, for 4 to 5 minutes. Stir in broccoli. Serve with Sesame Wheat Noodles. Makes 4 servings.

PER SERVING		DAILY GOAL
Calories	155	2,000 (F), 2,500 (M)
Total Fat	4 g	60 g or less (F), 70 g or less (M)
Saturated fat	1 g	20 g or less (F), 23 g or less (M)
Cholesterol	49 mg	300 mg or less
Sodium	673 mg	2,400 mg or less
Carbohydrates	8 g	250 g or more
Protein	23 g	55 g to 90 g

SESAME WHEAT NOODLES

▼ *Low-fat*
▽ *Low-calorie*
   Prep time: 5 minutes
   Cooking time: 15 minutes
○ *Degree of difficulty: easy*

8 **ounces whole-wheat spaghetti**
1 **tablespoon vegetable oil**
⅓ **cup finely chopped green onions**
1 **teaspoon minced garlic**
⅛ **teaspoon red pepper flakes**
1 **tablespoon reduced-sodium soy sauce**
1 **tablespoon toasted sesame seed**

1 Cook the spaghetti according to package directions; drain.

2 Heat the oil in a saucepan over medium-high heat. Add the green onions, garlic, and red pepper flakes. Cook 30 seconds; remove from heat. Stir in hot spaghetti, soy sauce, and sesame seed. Makes 4 servings.

PER SERVING		DAILY GOAL
Calories	245	2,000 (F), 2,500 (M)
Total Fat	5 g	60 g or less (F), 70 g or less (M)
Saturated fat	1 g	20 g or less (F), 23 g or less (M)
Cholesterol	0 mg	300 mg or less
Sodium	157 mg	2,400 mg or less
Carbohydrates	44 g	250 g or more
Protein	9 g	55 g to 90 g

TROPICAL CHICKEN WITH BROWN RICE

Mango chutney and diced fresh mango make a simple but unusual sauce for chicken. While the rice is on the stove and the chicken is in the microwave, steam some green beans or broccoli to complete the menu.

Ⓜ *Microwave*
   Prep time: 10 minutes
   Cooking time: 10 minutes
◯ *Degree of difficulty: easy*

¼ **cup mango chutney**
4 **teaspoons balsamic vinegar**
¼ **teaspoon coriander**
¼ **teaspoon cumin**
¼ **teaspoon ginger**
¼ **cup olive oil**
1 **packet boil-in-bag brown rice (4 ounces), uncooked**
1 **pound boneless, skinless chicken breasts**
¼ **teaspoon salt**
¼ **teaspoon freshly ground pepper**

1 **mango (about 1 pound) peeled and diced into ½-inch pieces, for garnish**
2 **tablespoons chopped green onions Mango slices, for garnish**
½ **cup toasted, slivered almonds, for garnish**

1 Combine chutney, balsamic vinegar, coriander, cumin, and ginger in a blender; blend until smooth. With machine on, slowly add oil through the opening in the top. Set the sauce aside.

2 Cook the rice according to package directions.

3 Meanwhile, season the chicken with salt and pepper. Place in a 9-inch square glass microwave-proof baking dish and cover with wax paper. Microwave on high (100% power) for 4 minutes. Rearrange chicken and pour sauce over. Cover and microwave on high (100% power) for 4 minutes more.

4 To serve, arrange chicken breasts on top of the brown rice on a platter. Spoon cooking juices over rice and garnish with mango, green onions, and almonds. Makes 4 servings.

PER SERVING		DAILY GOAL
Calories	550	2,000 (F), 2,500 (M)
Total Fat	24 g	60 g or less (F), 70 g or less (M)
Saturated fat	3 g	20 g or less (F), 23 g or less (M)
Cholesterol	66 mg	300 mg or less
Sodium	389 mg	2,400 mg or less
Carbohydrates	49 g	250 g or more
Protein	32 g	55 g to 90 g

NOTES

BALSAMIC CHICKEN BREASTS

In Modena, Italy, where balsamic vinegar is made, a bride is praised for the aged vinegar she can bring to the marriage. You'll be just as highly praised when you serve this delicious dish at home.

▼ *Low-fat*
Prep time: 10 minutes
Cooking time: 16 minutes
O *Degree of difficulty: easy*

4 **boneless, skinless chicken breast halves (about 1 pound)**
½ **teaspoon salt**
¼ **teaspoon freshly ground pepper**
1 **tablespoon olive oil**
¼ **cup minced shallots**
½ **cup chicken broth**
3 **tablespoons balsamic vinegar**
1 **teaspoon brown sugar**
1 **tablespoon butter *or* margarine**
1 **cup orzo pasta, cooked**
2 **tablespoons minced fresh parsley**

1 Place the chicken between 2 sheets of wax paper. Pound to ½ inch thick with rolling pin or mallet. Sprinkle chicken with the salt and pepper. Heat the oil in a large skillet over medium-high heat. Cook chicken about 4 minutes per side, until opaque in center. Transfer to a serving plate; cover and keep warm.

2 Add the shallots to skillet and cook, stirring, for 2 minutes. Carefully add the chicken broth, vinegar, and brown sugar. Bring to a boil; cook until reduced by one third, about 4 minutes. Whisk the butter or margarine into skillet until melted. Pour over chicken.

3 Toss the orzo with the parsley and serve with chicken. Makes 4 servings.

PER SERVING		DAILY GOAL
Calories	385	2,000 (F), 2,500 (M)
Total Fat	9 g	60 g or less (F), 70 g or less (M)
Saturated fat	3 g	20 g or less (F), 23 g or less (M)
Cholesterol	74 mg	300 mg or less
Sodium	527 mg	2,400 mg or less
Carbohydrates	41 g	250 g or more
Protein	33 g	55 g to 90 g

GARLICKY CHICKEN WINGS

These wings are not for the faint of heart.

Prep time: 10 minutes
Cooking time: 15 to 20 minutes
O *Degree of difficulty: easy*

2½ **pounds chicken wings**
1 **tablespoon olive oil**
1 **tablespoon butter *or* margarine**
1 **tablespoon minced garlic**
3 **tablespoons fresh lemon juice**
1 **tablespoon chopped fresh parsley**
½ **teaspoon salt**
½ **teaspoon freshly ground pepper**

1 Preheat broiler. Arrange the chicken wings in a single layer on a broiler rack. Broil, 4 inches from heat, for 10 minutes.

2 Meanwhile, heat the oil and butter in a small skillet over medium heat. Add the garlic and sauté until golden, about 2 to 3 minutes; strain. Add the lemon juice, salt, and pepper.

3 Brush chicken with half of the flavored oil. Broil about 10 to 15 minutes, turning once, or until crispy. Just before serving, brush with the remaining oil. Makes 4 servings.

PER SERVING		DAILY GOAL
Calories	373	2,000 (F), 2,500 (M)
Total Fat	27 g	60 g or less (F), 70 g or less (M)
Saturated fat	8 g	20 g or less (F), 23 g or less (M)
Cholesterol	98 mg	300 mg or less
Sodium	392 mg	2,400 mg or less
Carbohydrates	2 g	250 g or more
Protein	29 g	55 g to 90 g

NOTES

97

CHICKEN CURRY IN A HURRY

Boneless, skinless chicken breasts are interchangeable with the thighs in this recipe, but remember, thighs take a bit longer to cook. We've added just a touch of tomato paste to enhance the color and flavor of this curry sauce.

▼ *Low-fat*
Prep time: 10 minutes
Cooking time: 16 to 19 minutes
○ *Degree of difficulty: easy*

- 2 **tablespoons curry powder**
- 1 **teaspoon cumin**
- ¾ **teaspoon salt**
- ¼ **teaspoon freshly ground pepper**
  Pinch cloves
- 2 **tablespoons water**
- 1 **teaspoon minced garlic**
- 1 **teaspoon tomato paste**
- 1 **tablespoon vegetable oil**
- 2 **cups finely chopped onions**
- 8 **boneless, skinless chicken thighs (1¼ pounds), halved**
- 1 **Golden Delicious apple, cored, cut into 1-inch pieces**
- 1 **cup sliced carrots, cut into ½-inch pieces**
- ¾ **cup chicken broth**
- 1 **cup frozen peas, thawed**
- 1 **cup long-grain rice *or* couscous, cooked**

1 Combine the curry powder, cumin, salt, pepper, cloves, water, garlic, and tomato paste in a small bowl. Stir until blended; set aside.

2 Heat the oil in a Dutch oven over high heat. Add the onions and cook, stirring occasionally, until tender, about 3 to 4 minutes. Add the spice mixture, cook until fragrant, about 1 minute.

3 Add the chicken, apple, carrots, and broth. Reduce heat and simmer covered, stirring occasionally, until chicken is cooked and vegetables are tender, about 12 to 14 minutes. Stir in the peas and heat through. Serve with cooked rice or couscous. Makes 4 servings.

PER SERVING		DAILY GOAL
Calories	485	2,000 (F), 2,500 (M)
Total Fat	11 g	60 g or less (F), 70 g or less (M)
Saturated fat	2 g	20 g or less (F), 23 g or less (M)
Cholesterol	118 mg	300 mg or less
Sodium	814 mg	2,400 mg or less
Carbohydrates	61 g	250 g or more
Protein	35 g	55 g to 90 g

NOTES

MOROCCAN CHICKEN CUTLETS

This aromatic dish, loaded with chunky vegetables and chick-peas, goes from skillet to table in thirty minutes.

▼ *Low-fat*
▽ *Low-calorie*
  Prep time: 15 minutes
  Cooking time: 15 minutes
○ *Degree of difficulty: easy*

1 **tablespoon vegetable oil**
1½ **pounds chicken cutlets, about ½-inch thick**
½ **teaspoon salt**
½ **teaspoon freshly ground pepper**
½ **chopped onion**
1 **teaspoon minced garlic**
¼ **teaspoon ginger**
¼ **teaspoon cumin**
¼ **teaspoon turmeric**
⅛ **teaspoon cinnamon**
⅛ **teaspoon ground red pepper**
1 **can (13¾ or 14½ ounces) chicken broth**
4 **carrots, thinly sliced**
1 **cup canned chick-peas, rinsed and drained**
1 **pound zucchini, halved lengthwise and sliced ¼-inch thick**
  Hot cooked rice

1 Heat the oil in a large skillet over medium-high heat. Sprinkle both sides of the chicken cutlets with salt and pepper. Add half of the cutlets to skillet and sauté until just cooked through, about 1½ to 2 minutes per side. Transfer to serving platter and keep warm in oven. Repeat with remaining cutlets.

2 Add the onion to skillet; cook, stirring frequently, for 3 minutes. Stir in the garlic, ginger, cumin, turmeric, cinnamon, and red pepper and cook for 30 seconds. Carefully add the chicken broth, carrots, and chick-peas. Bring to a boil; cover and cook for 5 minutes.

3 Stir in the zucchini and cook covered just until tender, about 2 minutes more. Spoon vegetables over chicken. Serve with rice. Makes 4 servings.

PER SERVING		DAILY GOAL
Calories	340	2,000 (F), 2,500 (M)
Total Fat	8 g	60 g or less (F), 70 g or less (M)
Saturated fat	1 g	20 g or less (F), 23 g or less (M)
Cholesterol	99 mg	300 mg or less
Sodium	1,006 mg	2,400 mg or less
Carbohydrates	20 g	250 g or more
Protein	45 g	55 g to 90 g

NOTES

_____

_____

_____

_____

_____

_____

_____

_____

_____

_____

_____

_____

ANY WAY YOU CUT IT CHICKEN TASTES GREAT

Chicken is the ultimate convenience food, available in myriad sizes and cuts. Here are some guidelines on how best to use every bit of this versatile bird.

Whole broiler-fryer: The most popular size and economical variety of bird. The weight of these chickens can range anywhere from 2 to 4 pounds. (A "heavy broiler" weights 4½ to 5 lbs.) Great for roasting or poaching.

Young roaster or roasting chicken: This large, meaty bird weighs in between 5 and 8 pounds and is best suited for stuffing and roasting. Also great when poached in homemade soups or when preparing cooked chicken for salads or fillings.

Cut up chicken: Perhaps the most versatile variety of chicken. A whole broiler-fryer is cut into 8 pieces: 2 breast halves, 2 thighs, 2 drumsticks and 2 wings. A cut up chicken is ideal for broiling, frying, baking, grilling, or stewing.

Halves or splits: A whole broiler-fryer is cut into 2 equal pieces. For a knock-out presentation, have your butcher simply split the chicken down the backbone only, flattening the bird and leaving the whole breast intact. Either cut is ideal for broiling or grilling.

Quarters: Available as leg quarters or breast quarters, usually packaged separately and featuring all dark or white meat. An economical cut, great for baking, broiling, or grilling.

Legs: For dark meat lovers. This flavorful cut features the unseparated drumstick and thigh. It can easily be substituted for cut up chicken in any recipe.

Breast halves or split breasts: The most popular cut of chicken; all white meat. Boneless, skinless chicken breasts are ideal when trimming calories and fat. Perfect for stir-frying, poached for cooked chicken in salads, or pounded into cutlets, then sautéed or grilled.

Thighs: Increasingly popular when boned and skinned, this cut of dark meat is a wonderful alternative to boneless, skinless chicken breasts, though you'll need to increase the cooking time for proper doneness. (Boneless chicken parts should be cooked to 160°F.) Bone-in thighs can also be substituted for cut up chicken in any recipe.

Wings: The whole wing is composed of white meat. Economical, ideal for hors d'oeuvres and snacks, and best when grilled or broiled until crispy. Trim the wing tips if desired.

Ground chicken: A low-fat, low-calorie alternative to ground beef, and perfect for hamburgers or meatloaf. Made from boneless, skinless thigh meat. It can also be substituted for ground turkey.

CAJUN CHICKEN SANDWICH

Peppery chicken cutlets are cooled down with lemon mayonnaise and crisp lettuce on hearty bread.

Prep time: 15 minutes
Cooking time: 6 minutes
○ *Degree of difficulty: easy*

½ **cup mayonnaise**
1 **tablespoon chopped fresh parsley**
1 **teaspoon fresh lemon juice**
½ **teaspoon grated lemon peel**
½ **teaspoon salt**
½ **teaspoon freshly ground pepper**
½ **teaspoon cumin**
¼ **teaspoon paprika**
¼ **teaspoon ground red pepper**
4 **chicken cutlets (1 pound), about ½-inch thick**
3 **tablespoons butter *or* margarine, melted**
8 **slices (½ inch thick) Italian bread from large round loaf, toasted**
4 **lettuce leaves**
8 **thin slices red onion**

1 Stir together the mayonnaise, parsley, lemon juice, and lemon peel in a small bowl.

2 Combine the salt, pepper, cumin, paprika, and red pepper in a wide shallow bowl. Add the chicken cutlets to the spice mixture; turn to coat, then brush both sides with melted butter. Place in a single layer on wax paper.

3 Heat a well-seasoned, large cast-iron skillet over medium-high heat just to smoking. Add half of the cutlets and sauté just until cooked through, about 2½ minutes per side. Transfer to a plate and cover to keep warm. Repeat with remaining cutlets.

4 Spread 1 tablespoon of the lemon-mayonnaise over each slice of bread; top 4 slices of bread with a lettuce leaf, 2 slices of onion, a chicken cutlet and the remaining slices of bread. Makes 4 servings.

PER SERVING		DAILY GOAL
Calories	567	2,000 (F), 2,500 (M)
Total Fat	34 g	60 g or less (F), 70 g or less (M)
Saturated fat	9 g	20 g or less (F), 23 g or less (M)
Cholesterol	105 mg	300 mg or less
Sodium	944 mg	2,400 mg or less
Carbohydrates	32 g	250 g or more
Protein	32 g	55 g to 90 g

CHICKEN BURGERS WITH CRANBERRY MAYONNAISE

You can substitute ground turkey for the chicken we've called for, and the burgers are just as tasty with cole slaw as they are with the cranberry-flavored topping.

Prep time: 5 minutes
Cooking time: 6 minutes
○ *Degree of difficulty: easy*

1 **pound ground chicken**
3 **tablespoons seasoned dry bread crumbs**
2 **tablespoons water**
¼ **teaspoon salt**
¼ **teaspoon freshly ground pepper**
   Pinch poultry seasoning
3 **tablespoons whole cranberry sauce**
1 **tablespoon mayonnaise**
4 **rolls, split and toasted**
4 **Boston lettuce leaves**

1 Preheat broiler. Combine the chicken, bread crumbs, water, salt, pepper, and poultry seasoning in a small bowl. Shape the chicken mixture into four ½-inch-thick patties. Broil 3 inches from heat source about 3 minutes per side until cooked through.

2 Meanwhile, combine the cranberry sauce and mayonnaise in a small bowl; mix well.

3 On the bottom half of each roll, layer a lettuce leaf, a chicken burger, and 1 tablespoon of cranberry mayonnaise. Cover with roll tops. Makes 4 servings.

PER SERVING		DAILY GOAL
Calories	410	2,000 (F), 2,500 (M)
Total Fat	15 g	60 g or less (F), 70 g or less (M)
Saturated fat	3 g	20 g or less (F), 23 g or less (M)
Cholesterol	92 mg	300 mg or less
Sodium	710 mg	2,400 mg or less
Carbohydrates	39 g	250 g or more
Protein	26 g	55 g to 90 g

103

WARM CHICKEN AND PESTO VEGETABLE SANDWICH

You'll love this crunchy sweet pepper, radish, and carrot slaw on top of warm chicken cutlets. Using prepared pesto makes the dressing a snap.

▼ *Low-fat*
   Prep time: 10 minutes
   Cooking time: 4 to 6 minutes
○ *Degree of difficulty: easy*

1 **green onion, chopped**
¼ **cup sour cream**
2 **tablespoons prepared pesto**
1 **teaspoon fresh lemon juice**
¼ **teaspoon salt**
½ **red pepper, julienned**
½ **yellow pepper, julienned**
¼ **cup julienned radish**
¼ **cup shredded carrot**
1 **green onion, julienned**
4 **chicken cutlets (½ pound), about**
     ½-inch thick
8 **slices pumpernickle *or* black bread**

1 In a food processor puree chopped green onion, sour cream, pesto, lemon juice, and salt. Combine with the sweet peppers, radish, carrot, and julienned green onion in a bowl.

2 Spray a large skillet with vegetable cooking spray and heat over medium-high heat. Add the cutlets and sauté, turning once, until cooked through, about 4 to 6 minutes.

3 Place each cutlet on a slice of bread. Spoon the vegetable mixture over cutlets and top with remaining bread. Makes 4 servings.

PER SERVING		DAILY GOAL
Calories	365	2,000 (F), 2,500 (M)
Total Fat	10 g	60 g or less (F), 70 g or less (M)
Saturated fat	3 g	20 g or less (F), 23 g or less (M)
Cholesterol	73 mg	300 mg or less
Sodium	697 mg	2,400 mg or less
Carbohydrates	34 g	250 g or more
Protein	33 g	55 g to 90 g

NOTES

105

CHICKEN WITH

CRUNCH

Juicy on the inside, and crunchy on the outside... chicken doesn't get any better than this. So go ahead, sink your teeth into our Super Crunch Batter-Fried Chicken, Baked Cornflake Crunch Chicken, or indulge, guilt-free, in a skillet-fried Southern Buttermilk Chicken that's lower in calories.

NEW ORLEANS PECAN CHICKEN

In this nutty baked chicken, there's a Cajun spice bonus in every crunchy bite.

Prep time: 20 minutes
Cooking time: 30 to 35 minutes
O *Degree of difficulty: easy*

1½ **cups pecan halves**
⅓ **cup plain dry bread crumbs**
¾ **teaspoon salt**
¾ **teaspoon paprika**
½ **teaspoon oregano**
½ **teaspoon ground white pepper**
¼ **teaspoon ground red pepper**
½ **cup low-fat buttermilk**
1 **chicken (3 pounds), cut up**
2 **tablespoons butter *or* margarine, melted**

1 Preheat oven to 400°F. Grease a 13x9-inch baking pan.

2 Combine the pecans, bread crumbs, salt, paprika, oregano, and peppers in a food processor; process until nuts are chopped. Transfer to a plastic bag.

3 Pour the buttermilk into a medium bowl; dip the chicken into buttermilk, then add to the bag with pecan mixture and shake. Arrange chicken in the pan in a single layer; drizzle with butter. Bake for 30 to 35 minutes. Makes 4 servings.

PER SERVING		DAILY GOAL
Calories	740	2,000 (F), 2,500 (M)
Total Fat	55 g	60 g or less (F), 70 g or less (M)
Saturated fat	12 g	20 g or less (F), 23 g or less (M)
Cholesterol	151 mg	300 mg or less
Sodium	712 mg	2,400 mg or less
Carbohydrates	16 g	250 g or more
Protein	46 g	55 g to 90 g

NOTES

BATTER DIPPED CHICKEN NUGGETS WITH SWEET-AND-SOUR ORANGE SAUCE

Beer is the secret ingredient that gives this batter-coated chicken its super light and crunchy coating.

▼ *Low-fat*
 Prep time: 5 minutes
 Cooking time: 20 minutes
○ *Degree of difficulty: easy*

Vegetable oil for frying
1 cup all-purpose flour
1 teaspoon paprika
1 teaspoon salt
½ teaspoon freshly ground pepper
1 cup beer
1¼ pounds boneless, skinless chicken breasts, cubed

Orange Sauce
½ cup orange marmalade
1 to 2 tablespoons sugar
1 tablespoon white vinegar
1 tablespoon soy sauce
1 teaspoon grated fresh ginger
1 garlic clove, pressed
⅛ teaspoon red pepper flakes

1 Heat 2 inches of oil in a large skillet to 375°F. Combine the flour, paprika, salt, and pepper in a medium bowl. Whisk in the beer until smooth.

2 Dip the chicken in batter a few pieces at a time and fry, turning occasionally until golden, about 4 minutes. Drain on paper towels and keep warm. Repeat with remaining chicken and batter. Serve with Orange Sauce. Makes 4 servings.

Orange Sauce: In a blender combine the orange marmalade, sugar, white vinegar, soy sauce, ginger, garlic clove, and red pepper flakes. Process until well blended. Makes about ⅔ cup.

PER SERVING WITH
ONE TABLESPOON
ORANGE SAUCE

		DAILY GOAL
Calories	460	2,000 (F), 2,500 (M)
Total Fat	11 g	60 g or less (F), 70 g or less (M)
Saturated fat	2	20 g or less (F), 23 g or less (M)
Cholesterol	82 mg	300 mg or less
Sodium	787 mg	2,400 mg or less
Carbohydrates	52 g	250 g or more
Protein	36 g	55 g to 90 g

109

SUPER CRUNCH BATTER-FRIED CHICKEN

This extra-crispy chicken is perfect in any picnic basket. The secret to its super crunchy crust is self-rising flour! *Also pictured on page 106.*

Prep time: 10 minutes plus standing
Cooking time: 1 hour
O *Degree of difficulty: easy*

1½ **cups self-rising flour**
1 **cup low-fat buttermilk**
1 **chicken (3 pounds), cut up**
½ **teaspoon salt**
½ **teaspoon freshly ground pepper**
½ **teaspoon freshly grated nutmeg**
2 **cups vegetable shortening**

1 Place the flour in a large bowl and pour the buttermilk into another large bowl. Dip the chicken first in flour, then in buttermilk, shaking off any excess. Roll chicken in flour again, then place skin side up on a plate. Sprinkle with salt, pepper, and nutmeg. Let stand for 15 minutes.

2 Melt the shortening in a heavy, 10-inch skillet over medium heat to 350°F. Carefully add half of the chicken, cover and cook for 10 minutes.

3 Uncover and cook, turning once, until crisp and juices run clear when the chicken is pierced with a fork, about 20 minutes more. Drain on paper towels. Keep warm. Repeat with remaining chicken. Makes 6 servings.

PER SERVING		DAILY GOAL	
Calories	450	2,000 (F), 2,500 (M)	
Total Fat	30 g	60 g or less (F), 70 g or less (M)	
Saturated fat	8 g	20 g or less (F), 23 g or less (M)	
Cholesterol	116 mg	300 mg or less	
Sodium	418 mg	2,400 mg or less	
Carbohydrates	13 g	250 g or more	
Protein	31 g	55 g to 90 g	

NOTES

_____
_____
_____
_____
_____
_____
_____
_____
_____
_____
_____
_____
_____
_____
_____
_____
_____
_____

SOUTHERN BUTTERMILK CHICKEN

In this crispy skillet chicken with buttermilk gravy, we've cut the fat and calories but kept the flavor you love.

Prep time: 10 minutes
Cooking time: 25 to 30 minutes
○ *Degree of difficulty: easy*

4 **large chicken thighs (about 2 pounds)**
¾ **teaspoon salt**
¼ **teaspoon freshly ground pepper**
¼ **cup all-purpose flour**
2 **tablespoons vegetable oil, divided**
1¼ **cups low-fat buttermilk**
4 **bunches green onions, cut into 3-inch pieces**

1 Combine chicken, salt, pepper, and flour on a large plate; toss lightly to coat. Heat 1 tablespoon of the oil in a large skillet over high heat. Add chicken and cook until golden on all sides, 5 to 8 minutes. Remove chicken, discard excess oil.

2 Return skillet to heat and add buttermilk, scraping pan to loosen any browned bits. Add chicken, skin side up. Reduce heat, cover and simmer until chicken is tender and juices run clear when the chicken is pierced with a fork, 15 to 20 minutes.

3 Heat the remaining oil in another skillet over high heat. Add green onions; toss to coat. Cook until golden, 2 to 3 minutes.

4 Transfer chicken and green onions to a warm serving platter. Pour remaining juices into blender and blend until smooth. Serve with chicken. Makes 4 servings.

PER SERVING		DAILY GOAL
Calories	535	2,000 (F), 2,500 (M)
Total Fat	35 g	60 g or less (F), 70 g or less (M)
Saturated fat	9 g	20 g or less (F), 23 g or less (M)
Cholesterol	154 mg	300 mg or less
Sodium	773 mg	2,400 mg or less
Carbohydrates	18 g	250 g or more
Protein	37 g	55 g to 90 g

THE WAY TO CRUNCH: A GUIDE TO THE PERFECT FRIED CHICKEN

There are countless ways to enjoy the great flavor of fried chicken. Leave the skin on or take it off...Dip the chicken in egg, buttermilk, or nothing at all...Toss your bird with seasoned flour, crumbs or nuts...Fry it in vegetable shortening, oil, butter, or even in bacon grease. You can get the crispy skin we all love if you follow these few simple guidelines. Here's how:

1 Always use a large enough skillet, preferably heavy-bottomed or cast iron. For one cut up chicken, the ideal size is at least 10 inches, and preferably 12 to 14 inches, so the pieces are never crowded in the pan. If that size is not available, use 2 smaller skillets or cook your chicken in batches.

2 Whether you choose oil, shortening, butter or a combination, before adding the chicken to the skillet, the frying oil must always be fully preheated to the proper temperature, 350°F. If you don't have a deep-fat thermometer, drop a cube of white bread into the preheated oil. Bubbles should immediately appear

PISTACHIO CHICKEN CUTLETS

We guarantee this "flash in the pan" chicken to stay crisp, nutty, and crunchy on the outside, moist and juicy on the inside. Try serving mashed sweet potatoes for a colorful side dish.

Prep time: 10 minutes
Cooking time: 4 to 6 minutes
Degree of difficulty: easy

6 tablespoons all-purpose flour, divided

1 pound chicken cutlets, about ½ inch thick
1 large egg
½ cup unsalted shelled pistachios *or* almonds
1 teaspoon salt
½ teaspoon freshly ground pepper
¼ cup butter *or* margarine
Lemon wedges, for garnish

1 Place 2 tablespoons of the flour on a plate. Coat the chicken cutlets with flour and shake off any excess. Place cutlets in a single layer on wax paper or a wire rack.

2 Lightly beat the egg in a shallow bowl. Process the remaining 4 tablespoons of flour with the pistachios or almonds, salt, and pepper in blender until finely chopped; transfer to a shallow bowl.

3 Heat the butter in a 12-inch skillet over medium-high heat. Dip one cutlet at a time in egg, coat with pistachio mixture and add to skillet. Sauté cutlets until golden brown, about 2 to 3 minutes per side. Drain on paper towels. Garnish with lemon wedges.

PER SERVING		DAILY GOAL
Calories	380	2,000 (F), 2,500 (M)
Total Fat	22 g	60 g or less (F), 70 g or less (M)
Saturated fat	9 g	20 g or less (F), 23 g or less (M)
Cholesterol	150 mg	300 mg or less
Sodium	760 mg	2,400 mg or less
Carbohydrates	13 g	250 g or more
Protein	32 g	55 g to 90 g

around the bread and it should brown in 1 minute. If the oil is too hot, the chicken will brown too quickly and overcook outside before the inside is done. If the oil is not hot enough, the chicken will take too long to cook, absorb too much oil, and become greasy.

3 Whether or not you choose to cover your skillet during frying, the amount of frying oil should never come more than a third of the way up the sides of the chicken pieces. Fry the chicken pieces over medium heat, turning the pieces only once with metal tongs. Do not use a fork or you will pierce the flesh and lose any natural juices. Once the chicken is fried, transfer the pieces to paper towels to drain. Serve hot, room temperature or cold.

4 To prepare chicken in an electric deep fat fryer, fill the fryer with oil as directed (the suggested depth is about 1½ inches). Heat the oil to 350°F. Cook the chicken in batches without crowding it. Deep fat frying cooks the chicken faster, so check it for doneness after 15 minutes.

OVEN-FRIED CHICKEN BOMBAY

Boneless chicken thighs have become more popular, in answer to the growing demand for quick-cooking chicken products. Pounded to a uniform thickness, this Indian-spiced chicken cooks up fast and crispy. A refreshing yogurt sauce cools it down.

Prep time: 15 minutes
Cooking time: 17 to 20 minutes
O *Degree of difficulty: easy*

½ **cup plain dry bread crumbs**
1 **tablespoon butter** *or* **margarine, melted**
4 **large boneless, skinless chicken thighs (about 2 pounds)**
1 **teaspoon paprika**
½ **teaspoon cumin**
½ **teaspoon coriander**
½ **teaspoon salt**
¼ **teaspoon ginger**
⅛ **teaspoon ground red pepper**
 Half of 1 lemon

Yogurt Sauce
1 **container (8 ounces) plain low-fat yogurt**
½ **cup fresh cilantro leaves**
¼ **cup fresh mint leaves**
1 **teaspoon fresh lemon juice**
¼ **teaspoon salt**
 Pinch ground red pepper
 Steamed rice

1 Preheat oven to 425°F. Combine the bread crumbs and melted butter in a small bowl; toss to combine. Set aside.

2 Between 2 sheets of wax paper, pound the chicken thighs lightly to ½-inch thick. In a small bowl, combine the paprika, cumin, coriander, salt, ginger, and red pepper. Rub mixture on both sides of each chicken piece. Lightly squeeze a few drops of lemon juice over each piece, then dip into the crumbs to coat both sides evenly.

3 Place on a cookie sheet and bake about 17 to 20 minutes, until juices run clear. Serve with yogurt sauce and steamed rice. Makes 4 servings.

Yogurt Sauce: While the chicken is baking, combine the yogurt, cilantro, mint, lemon juice, salt, and red pepper in a blender; puree just until smooth. Makes about 1 cup.

PER SERVING		DAILY GOAL
Calories	385	2,000 (F), 2,500 (M)
Total Fat	13 g	60 g or less (F), 70 g or less (M)
Saturated fat	5 g	20 g or less (F), 23 g or less (M)
Cholesterol	200 mg	300 mg or less
Sodium	766 mg	2,400 mg or less
Carbohydrates	14 g	250 g or more
Protein	49 g	55 g to 90 g

NOTES

CORNFLAKE CRUNCH CHICKEN

Crushed cornflakes seasoned with herbs give this oven-fried chicken the crispiest skin ever using only a fraction of the fat!

▼ *Low-fat*
▽ *Low-calorie*
   Prep time: 5 minutes
   Cooking time: 20 minutes
○ *Degree of difficulty: easy*

¾ **cup finely crushed cornflakes**
½ **teaspoon basil**
½ **teaspoon garlic powder**
½ **teaspoon freshly ground pepper**
¼ **teaspoon salt**
¼ **teaspoon oregano**
1 **large egg**
2 **whole boneless, skinless chicken breasts (1 pound), split**
1 **tablespoon butter *or* margarine, melted**

1 Preheat oven to 400°F. Combine the cornflakes, basil, garlic powder, pepper, salt, and oregano in a shallow bowl. Lightly beat the egg in another shallow bowl.

2 Dip the chicken in the egg, then in the cornflakes.

3 Place chicken on a wire rack in a shallow baking pan. Drizzle with the melted butter. Bake for 20 minutes. Makes 4 servings.

PER SERVING		DAILY GOAL
Calories	255	2,000 (F), 2,500 (M)
Total Fat	6 g	60 g or less (F), 70 g or less (M)
Saturated fat	3 g	20 g or less (F), 23 g or less (M)
Cholesterol	127 mg	300 mg or less
Sodium	516 mg	2,400 mg or less
Carbohydrates	19 g	250 g or more
Protein	30 g	55 g to 90 g

BAKED SESAME CHICKEN WITH GINGER

Chicken cutlets can be substituted for boneless thighs in this Asian-inspired entrée, which is perfect with stir-fried vegetables.

   Prep time: 5 minutes
   Cooking time: 20 minutes
○ *Degree of difficulty: easy*

1 **large egg**
2 **tablespoons soy sauce**
½ **cup plain dry bread crumbs**
¼ **cup sesame seed**
1½ **teaspoons ginger**
1¼ **pounds boneless, skinless chicken thighs**
3 **tablespoons butter *or* margarine, melted**

1 Preheat oven to 400°F. Beat the egg with the soy sauce in a shallow bowl. Combine the bread crumbs, sesame seed, and ginger in another bowl.

2 Dip the chicken in egg mixture, then in crumbs.

3 Place chicken on a wire rack in a shallow baking pan. Drizzle with the melted butter. Bake for 20 minutes. Makes 4 servings.

PER SERVING		DAILY GOAL
Calories	375	2,000 (F), 2,500 (M)
Total Fat	21 g	60 g or less (F), 70 g or less (M)
Saturated fat	8 g	20 g or less (F), 23 g or less (M)
Cholesterol	194 mg	300 mg or less
Sodium	857 mg	2,400 mg or less
Carbohydrates	13 g	250 g or more
Protein	33 g	55 g to 90 g

CRISPY CHICKEN SCALOPPINE

A fresh bread crumb coating with garlic and parsley lightens up this Italian classic, but we've kept the crunch by flash broiling the chicken. Serve with any short pasta or orzo.

▼ *Low-calorie*
Prep time: 15 minutes
Cooking time: 6 minutes
○ *Degree of difficulty: easy*

1 **large egg white**
2 **tablespoons water**
1 **cup fresh bread crumbs**
2 **tablespoons chopped fresh parsley**
1 **teaspoon minced garlic**
¼ **teaspoon freshly ground pepper**
2 **whole boneless, skinless chicken breasts (1 pound), split and pounded thin**
   Salt
4 **thin slices prosciutto ham (1½ ounces total)**
2 **tablespoons olive oil, divided**
   Lemon wedges

1 Preheat broiler. Whisk the egg white and water together in a shallow dish. Combine the bread crumbs, parsley, garlic, and pepper in another shallow dish.

2 Season chicken lightly with salt. Press 1 slice of prosciutto on each piece of chicken. Dip in egg white mixture, then in crumbs. Place on a broiler rack; sprinkle with 1 tablespoon of the oil.

3 Broil for 3 minutes; turn and sprinkle with the remaining 1 tablespoon oil. Broil about 3 minutes more until the chicken is firm to the touch and just opaque in the center. Serve with lemon wedges. Makes 4 servings.

PER SERVING		DAILY GOAL
Calories	245	2,000 (F), 2,500 (M)
Total Fat	10 g	60 g or less (F), 70 g or less (M)
Saturated fat	2 g	20 g or less (F), 23 g or less (M)
Cholesterol	75 mg	300 mg or less
Sodium	340 mg	2,400 mg or less
Carbohydrates	6 g	250 g or more
Protein	31 g	55 g to 90 g

PERFECT CHICKEN CUTLETS: IT'S ALL ABOUT POUNDING

It's easy and more economical to pound your own boneless, skinless chicken breasts into convenient cutlets. Here's how:

Moisten both sides of a boneless, skinless chicken breast half with water and place, smooth side down, on a sheet of wax paper or plastic wrap. (Moistening the chicken will help prevent the paper from sticking to the meat.) Top the chicken with another sheet of wax paper or plastic wrap.

Starting at the center and working toward the edges, gently pound the chicken to the desired thickness with the flat side of a meat mallet. Peel off both sheets of paper and discard.

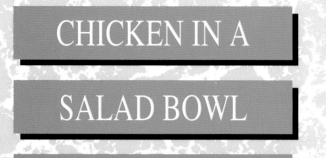

CHICKEN IN A
SALAD BOWL

Chicken is great hot or cold in a salad bowl. So, whether your bird's on ice with garlicky sesame noodles, piping hot off the grill, or tossed with spinach, fresh fruits, and ginger vinaigrette, each one of these delicious main-course salads will delight any chicken lover.

CHICKEN CAESAR SALAD

We made this Caesar salad a main dish by tossing the trademark garlic and anchovy dressing with grilled chicken. Rye bread makes for unusual, crunchy croutons.

Prep time: 35 minutes
Cooking time: 6 minutes
Degree of difficulty: easy

⅓ **cup plus 1 tablespoon olive oil**

2 **slices rye bread, crusts removed, cut into ½-inch cubes**

1 **pound boneless, skinless chicken breasts**

½ **teaspoon salt, divided**

½ **teaspoon freshly ground pepper, divided**

4 **anchovy fillets, chopped**

2 **teaspoons minced garlic**

2 **tablespoons fresh lemon juice**

1 **tablespoon Dijon mustard**

2 **dashes red pepper sauce**

1 **large head romaine lettuce, torn**

3 **tablespoons freshly grated Parmesan cheese**

1 Prepare grill or preheat broiler. Heat 1 tablespoon of the oil in a large skillet over medium-high heat. Add the bread cubes and cook, stirring occasionally, until lightly browned, about 5 minutes. Drain on paper towels and set aside.

2 Lightly oil the grill rack or broiler pan. Season the chicken breasts with ¼ teaspoon each of salt and pepper. Grill or broil 3 inches from heat, turning once. Cook through but still moist, about 5 to 6 minutes. Cool for 5 minutes, then cut crosswise into ¼-inch-thick slices.

3 Mash the anchovies, garlic, and the remaining ¼ teaspoon salt to a paste in a large salad bowl. Add the lemon juice, mustard, pepper sauce, and remaining ¼ teaspoon pepper; whisk until blended. Gradually whisk in the remaining ⅓ cup of oil. Add chicken and toss to coat. Add the lettuce, Parmesan, and rye croutons; toss well. Makes 4 servings.

PER SERVING		DAILY GOAL	
Calories	420	2,000 (F), 2,500 (M)	
Total Fat	26 g	60 g or less (F), 70 g or less (M)	
Saturated fat	5 g	20 g or less (F), 23 g or less (M)	
Cholesterol	72 mg	300 mg or less	
Sodium	802 mg	2,400 mg or less	
Carbohydrates	13 g	250 g or more	
Protein	33 g	55 g to 90 g	

CHICKEN TONNATO SALAD

This tuna-based sauce, from the classic veal tonnato, is an ideal topping for chicken and vegetables. Italian tuna packed in oil gives the most flavor and the smoothest texture.

Ⓜ *Microwave*
   Prep time: 35 minutes
   Microwave time: 10 minutes
Ⓞ *Degree of difficulty: easy*

¾ **pound boneless, skinless chicken breasts**
1 **pound tiny red potatoes, halved**
½ **pound green beans, trimmed**
½ **pound spinach leaves, trimmed**
2 **cups broccoli florets**
2 **cups cauliflower florets**
1 **yellow pepper, sliced**
2 **cups cherry tomatoes**

Tonnato Dressing
1 **can (6½ ounces) tuna packed in olive oil**
½ **cup mayonnaise**
6 **flat anchovy fillets packed in oil**
2 **tablespoons fresh lemon juice**
1 **tablespoon capers**
¼ **teaspoon freshly ground pepper**
1 **tablespoon chopped fresh parsley**

1 Bring 2 cups of salted water to simmer in a large skillet. Add the chicken, cover and cook until firm, about 10 minutes. Cool in the poaching liquid for 20 minutes. Remove chicken from liquid and slice thin.

2 Meanwhile, cover the potatoes and microwave in a 9-inch microwave-proof pie plate with 2 tablespoons of water on high (100% power) for 3 minutes, stir to rearrange. Microwave on high (100% power) for 3 minutes more or until tender. Rinse in a colander under cold water.

3 Place the beans with 1 tablespoon of water in the pie plate. Microwave covered on high (100% power) for 2 minutes, stir. Microwave on high (100% power) for 2 minutes more or until tender-crisp. Rinse under cold water.

4 Arrange chicken, potatoes, beans, spinach, broccoli, cauliflower, pepper, and tomatoes on each of 4 serving plates. Drizzle with the Tonnato Dressing. Serve any remaining dressing on the side. Makes 4 servings.

Tonnato Dressing: Process the tuna with the oil, mayonnaise, anchovies, lemon juice, capers, and pepper in a food processor until smooth. Stir in the parsley. Transfer to a bowl. Makes 1¼ cups.

PER SERVING		DAILY GOAL
Calories	560	2,000 (F), 2,500 (M)
Total Fat	30 g	60 g or less (F), 70 g or less (M)
Saturated fat	4 g	20 g or less (F), 23 g or less (M)
Cholesterol	87 mg	300 mg or less
Sodium	810 mg	2,400 mg or less
Carbohydrates	36 g	250 g or more
Protein	40 g	55 g to 90 g

NOTES

_____

_____

_____

_____

_____

_____

_____

_____

_____

WARM CHICKEN AND BLUE CHEESE SALAD WITH WALNUTS

This salad topped off with a warm bacon, shallot and cider dressing is perfect on a cold winter's day. *Also pictured on page 118.*

Prep time: 25 minutes
Cooking time: 20 minutes
○ *Degree of difficulty: easy*

4 ounces fresh spinach leaves (about 4 cups), rinsed, trimmed
4 ounces chicory (about 4 cups), torn
2 ounces radicchio (about 2 cups), torn *or* red cabbage, shredded
4 slices bacon, chopped
1 pound chicken cutlets, about ½-inch thick
3 tablespoons walnut halves
2 tablespoons minced shallots *or* onion
2 tablespoons cider vinegar
¼ cup olive oil
  Salt
  Freshly ground pepper

2 ounces Roquefort cheese (about ¼ cup), crumbled

1 Combine the spinach, chicory, and radicchio in a large salad bowl. Cook the bacon in a large skillet over medium-high heat until crisp. Drain bacon on paper towels. Pour off all but 2 tablespoons of the drippings in skillet. Add half the chicken cutlets and the walnuts; sauté just until chicken is cooked through, about 1½ to 2 minutes per side. Transfer chicken and walnuts to a plate; cover and keep warm.

2 Sauté remaining chicken. Reduce heat to medium. Add the shallots and cook, stirring frequently, until translucent, about 2 minutes. Pour in the vinegar and boil, scraping up any browned bits from the bottom of the pan. Remove from heat; whisk in the oil, and salt and pepper to taste. Pour over greens and toss to coat.

3 Slice chicken and fan slices over greens. Sprinkle with walnuts, bacon, and cheese. Makes 4 servings.

PER SERVING		DAILY GOAL
Calories	430	2,000 (F), 2,500 (M)
Total Fat	31 g	60 g or less (F), 70 g or less (M)
Saturated fat	8 g	20 g or less (F), 23 g or less (M)
Cholesterol	89 mg	300 mg or less
Sodium	501 mg	2,400 mg or less
Carbohydrates	5 g	250 g or more
Protein	33 g	55 g to 90 g

NOTES

GRILLED CHICKEN AND SPINACH SALAD

We've combined grilled chicken and oranges with the great flavors of a spinach-bacon salad, and the results are pure refreshment.

Prep time: 17 minutes
Cooking time: 8 to10 minutes
O *Degree of difficulty: easy*

2 **pounds fresh spinach, rinsed, trimmed**
¾ **cup thinly sliced red cabbage**
8 **thin slices red onion**
1 **orange, peeled and sectioned**
4 **boneless, skinless chicken breast halves (about 1 pound)**

Hot Bacon Dressing
3 **tablespoons brandy**
3 **tablespoons red wine vinegar**
1 **tablespoon soy sauce**
1 **teaspoon sugar**
¼ **teaspoon grated lemon peel**
¼ **teaspoon freshly ground pepper**
2 **slices bacon, halved**
3 **tablespoons vegetable oil**

1 Prepare grill or preheat broiler. Toss the spinach, cabbage, onion, and orange in a large bowl; set aside.

2 Grill the chicken over medium-hot coals or broil, 4 inches from heat, about 4 to 5 minutes per side until cooked through. Cool slightly.

3 Pour the Hot Bacon Dressing over the salad and toss to coat. Divide salad among 4 dinner plates; crumble on the bacon. Thinly slice each chicken breast and fan over each serving. Makes 4 servings.

Hot Bacon Dressing: Whisk brandy, vinegar, soy sauce, sugar, lemon peel, and pepper in a cup; set aside. Cook the bacon in a skillet over medium-high heat until crisp; drain. Discard all but 1 tablespoon of the drippings from skillet. Add the vinegar mixture and cook, stirring, for 45 seconds. Remove from heat; whisk in oil.

PER SERVING		DAILY GOAL
Calories	335	2,000 (F), 2,500 (M)
Total Fat	16 g	60 g or less (F), 70 g or less (M)
Saturated fat	3 g	20 g or less (F), 23 g or less (M)
Cholesterol	71 mg	300 mg or less
Sodium	465 mg	2,400 mg or less
Carbohydrates	11 g	250 g or more
Protein	30 g	55 g to 90 g

NOTES

GRILLED CHICKEN SALAD WITH SUMMER FRUIT

A warm weather delight! Smoky grilled chicken and fresh fruits are tossed in a ginger-lime dressing for an intriguing contrast of flavors and textures

▽ *Low-calorie*
Prep time: 15 minutes plus cooling
Cooking time: 10 minutes
O *Degree of difficulty: easy*

½ **teaspoon fennel seed**
4 **tablespoons vegetable oil, divided**
4 **tablespoons fresh lime juice,**
  divided
1 **teaspoon salt, divided**
¼ **teaspoon freshly ground pepper**
4 **chicken cutlets (8 ounces), about**
  ½-inch thick
⅛ **teaspoon red pepper flakes**
⅛ **teaspoon grated lime peel**
2 **nectarines, very thinly sliced**
2 **plums, very thinly sliced**
2 **green onions, minced**
2 **teaspoons grated fresh ginger**
3 **cups packed spinach leaves**
2 **cups watercress**
  Julienned lime peel, for garnish

1 Heat a skillet over medium-high heat; toast the fennel seed, shaking until fragrant, about 2 minutes. Crush seed with the back of a knife.

2 Combine 1 tablespoon of the oil, 1 tablespoon of the lime juice, ½ teaspoon of the salt, pepper, and fennel seed in a shallow bowl. Add the chicken; turn to coat. Cover and refrigerate.

3 Meanwhile, whisk the remaining 3 tablespoons oil, 1 tablespoon of lime juice, remaining ½ teaspoon salt, the pepper flakes, and the lime peel in a bowl. Toss the nectarines, plums, green onions, remaining 2 tablespoons lime juice, and the ginger together in another bowl.

4 Preheat grill for direct heat or broiler. Grill the chicken 4 inches from heat source, 4 minutes per side. Slice chicken into ½-inch wide strips. Toss the greens with lime dressing; place on a platter. Top with chicken and spoon on fruit. Garnish with lime peel. Makes 4 servings.

PER SERVING		DAILY GOAL
Calories	320	2,000 (F), 2,500 (M)
Total Fat	16 g	60 g or less (F), 70 g or less (M)
Saturated fat	2 g	20 g or less (F), 23 g or less (M)
Cholesterol	66 mg	300 mg or less
Sodium	671 mg	2,400 mg or less
Carbohydrates	17 g	250 g or more
Protein	29 g	55 g to 90 g

NOTES

CHINESE CHICKEN AND NOODLES

Eat your garlic and keep your friends. The soy, ginger, and sesame oil mask any hint of "garlic breath."

Prep time: 30 minutes
Cooking time: 10 minutes
○ *Degree of difficulty: easy*

- **1   pound linguine *or* thin spaghetti**
- **4   ounces snow peas**
- **½   teaspoon salt**
- **2   cups cooked, julienned chicken**
- **1   red pepper, julienned**
- **1   can (8 ounces) sliced water chestnuts *or* 1 large celery rib, thinly sliced**
- **½   cup thinly sliced green onions**
- **2   teaspoons sesame seed, toasted (optional)**

Gingered Dressing
- **⅓   cup vegetable oil**
- **⅓   cup soy sauce**
- **2   tablespoons honey**
- **1   teaspoon Oriental sesame oil**
- **½   teaspoon red pepper flakes**
- **½   cup coarsely chopped fresh ginger**
- **2   teaspoons finely chopped garlic**
- **2   tablespoons coarsely chopped green onion**

1 Cook the pasta according to package directions. Drain and rinse under cold water and set aside.

2 Heat the snow peas and salt in 1 inch of water in a medium saucepan over high heat until snow peas are bright green, about 20 seconds. Remove from heat. Drain and rinse under cold water. Julienne.

3 Add snow peas and pasta to the Gingered Dressing with the chicken, red pepper, water chestnuts, green onions, and sesame seed, if desired; toss to coat. (Can be made ahead. Cover and refrigerate up to 4 hours.) Makes 6 servings.

Gingered Dressing: Combine oil, soy sauce, honey, sesame oil, and pepper flakes in a large bowl. In a food processor, process ginger, garlic, and green onion until chopped fine. Whisk into soy mixture.

PER SERVING		DAILY GOAL
Calories	555	2,000 (F), 2,500 (M)
Total Fat	18 g	60 g or less (F), 70 g or less (M)
Saturated fat	3 g	20 g or less (F), 23 g or less (M)
Cholesterol	42 mg	300 mg or less
Sodium	147 mg	2,400 mg or less
Carbohydrates	73 g	250 g or more
Protein	25 g	55 g to 90 g

OUR BEST QUICK - COOKED CHICKEN

The next time you need some cooked chicken and have run out of leftovers, try this extra flavorful poached chicken that's ready in a flash.

Bring ½ cup of chicken broth or water, 1 tablespoon chopped fresh parsley, 2 teaspoons chopped shallots or onion, ¼ teaspoon thyme, and a pinch of freshly ground pepper to boil in a large skillet. Add 1 pound of chicken cutlets; reduce the heat and simmer for 3 minutes. Turn the chicken and simmer just until it is cooked through, about 4 to 5 minutes. Transfer with a slotted spoon to a cutting board. Cut as desired. Cover and refrigerate to chill. Makes 2 generous cups of cubed, cooked chicken.

CURRIED LENTIL SALAD WITH CHICKEN

A nice change from pasta, lentils are easy to cook, loaded with fiber, and compatible with many flavors. Seasoned with curry, served with poached chicken, and cooled with a yogurt-cilantro sauce, this salad is the perfect lunch on a steamy afternoon.

Prep time: 25 minutes plus cooling
Cooking time: 30 minutes
O *Degree of difficulty: easy*

1 cup lentils, picked over and rinsed
2 cups water
1 cinnamon stick (3 inches)
6 whole cloves
6 cardamom pods
2 tablespoons fresh lemon juice
2 tablespoons olive oil
1¼ teaspoons salt, divided
½ teaspoon curry powder
½ teaspoon freshly ground pepper
1 cup thinly sliced celery
¼ cup thinly sliced green onions
1 pound boneless, skinless chicken breasts

Seedless red grapes
¼ cup chopped, toasted almonds

Creamy Cilantro Sauce
½ cup plain low-fat yogurt
½ cup reduced-fat sour cream
½ cup fresh cilantro leaves, chopped
1 tablespoon fresh lemon juice
½ teaspoon salt
⅛ to ¼ teaspoon ground red pepper

1 Combine the lentils, water, cinnamon, cloves, and cardamom in a small saucepan. Bring to a boil. Reduce heat, cover and simmer until tender, about 20 minutes. Drain.

2 Whisk the lemon juice, oil, ¾ teaspoon of the salt, and the curry, and pepper in a small bowl. Add hot lentils and toss. Cool. Remove the whole spices and stir in the celery and green onions.

3 Meanwhile, combine the chicken with the remaining ½ teaspoon salt and water to cover in a medium saucepan. Bring almost to a boil. Reduce heat and simmer gently for 10 minutes. Drain, then cool to room temperature.

4 Slice chicken thin and arrange on a platter with lentils and grapes. Drizzle chicken with some of the Creamy Cilantro Sauce and sprinkle with almonds. Pass any remaining sauce. Makes 4 servings.

Creamy Cilantro Sauce: Combine the yogurt, sour cream, cilantro, lemon juice, salt, and red pepper all ingredients in a small bowl. Makes 1 cup.

PER SERVING		DAILY GOAL
Calories	475	2,000 (F), 2,500 (M)
Total Fat	17 g	60 g or less (F), 70 g or less (M)
Saturated fat	4 g	20 g or less (F), 23 g or less (M)
Cholesterol	78 mg	300 mg or less
Sodium	953 mg	2,400 mg or less
Carbohydrates	36 g	250 g or more
Protein	45 g	55 g to 90 g

NOTES

_____
_____
_____
_____
_____
_____
_____
_____

CHICKEN WALDORF SALAD

We've lightened up this classic salad by using low-fat yogurt, reduced-fat sour cream, and just a hint of grated orange peel.

▽ *Low-calorie*
   Prep time: 15 minutes plus chilling
○ *Degree of difficulty: easy*

¼ **cup plain low-fat yogurt**
1 **tablespoon reduced-fat sour cream**
½ **teaspoon grated orange peel**
¼ **teaspoon salt**
¼ **teaspoon freshly ground pepper**
½ **pound cooked chicken, skinned and diced**
1 **apple, cored, diced**
⅔ **cup diced celery**
⅓ **cup chopped green onions**
1 **tablespoon chopped toasted walnuts**
   Lettuce leaves

1 Combine the yogurt, sour cream, orange peel, salt, and pepper in a large bowl. Add the chicken, apple, celery, and green onion and toss well. Refrigerate 1 hour.

2 Line 4 serving plates with the lettuce leaves. Stir the walnuts into chicken mixture and divide evenly among plates. Makes 4 servings.

PER SERVING		DAILY GOAL
Calories	150	2,000 (F), 2,500 (M)
Total Fat	4 g	60 g or less (F), 70 g or less (M)
Saturated fat	1 g	20 g or less (F), 23 g or less (M)
Cholesterol	51 mg	300 mg or less
Sodium	208 mg	2,400 mg or less
Carbohydrates	8 g	250 g or more
Protein	19 g	55 g to 90 g

WARM CHICKEN SALAD WITH GOAT CHEESE

Have all the ingredients ready before you begin, so the chicken is still warm when you serve it on cool, crunchy salad greens.

   Prep time: 20 minutes
   Cooking time: 6 minutes
○ *Degree of difficulty: easy*

4 **cups torn Boston lettuce**
2½ **cups torn radicchio**
3 **cups arrugula**
½ **cup crumbled goat cheese**

3 **tablespoons olive oil, divided**
1 **pound boneless, skinless chicken breasts, cut into ½-inch strips**
⅓ **cup sliced shallots**
⅓ **cup walnut pieces**
1 **teaspoon salt, divided**
¼ **teaspoon freshly ground pepper**
⅛ **teaspoon thyme**
3 **tablespoons red wine vinegar**

1 Combine lettuce, radicchio, arrugula and goat cheese in a large salad bowl.

2 Heat 2 tablespoons of the oil in a large skillet over high heat. Add the chicken, shallots, walnuts, ½ teaspoon of the salt, pepper, and thyme; cook, stirring frequently, until chicken is just golden, 5 minutes. Transfer chicken to salad. Add remaining 1 tablespoons oil, the vinegar and remaining ½ teaspoon salt to hot skillet; stir. Pour over greens; toss well. Makes 4 servings.

PER SERVING		DAILY GOAL
Calories	390	2,000 (F), 2,500 (M)
Total Fat	25 g	60 g or less (F), 70 g or less (M)
Saturated fat	2 g	20 g or less (F), 23 g or less (M)
Cholesterol	66 mg	300 mg or less
Sodium	925 mg	2,400 mg or less
Carbohydrates	9 g	250 g or more
Protein	34 g	55 g to 90 g

CHICKEN WITH

FIRE AND SMOKE

No food tastes better cooked outdoors than chicken. Simply select from a perfect do-ahead citrus marinated Mediterranean Chicken with fresh herbs for entertaining, Firecracker Barbequed Chicken that lets your microwave take the chill off, or Caribbean Grilled Chicken flavored with a fragrant dry spice rub.

GRILLED PROVENÇAL CHICKEN

Our secret for flavorful grilled chicken is this fresh herb "dry rub" marinade, which is simply spread over the chicken and under the skin. For maximum taste, grill gently over indirect heat, making sure not to burn the skin.

Prep time: 15 minutes plus marinating
Grilling time: 25 to 35 minutes
○ *Degree of difficulty: easy*

5   **teaspoons fresh rosemary** *or*
    1½ teaspoons dried, crushed

1   **tablespoon chopped fresh thyme** *or*
    1 teaspoon dried, crushed
1   **tablespoon olive oil**
2   **teaspoons grated orange peel**
½   **teaspoon salt**
½   **teaspoon freshly ground pepper**
1   **chicken (3½ pounds), cut up**

1   Combine the rosemary, thyme, oil, orange peel, salt, and pepper in a small bowl. Rub mixture over the chicken and under the skin. Wrap and refrigerate overnight. Remove from refrigerator 1 hour before grilling.

2   Prepare grill for indirect heat. Place a disposable foil roasting pan in the bottom center of grill. Open all grill vents. Arrange 20 charcoal briquettes on each of 2 opposite sides of foil pan. Ignite charcoal.

3   When white ash has formed, grill chicken covered over medium-low coals about 25 to 35 minutes, turning every 5 minutes, until juices run clear when the chicken is pierced with a fork. Makes 4 servings.

PER SERVING		DAILY GOAL	
Calories	450	2,000 (F), 2,500 (M)	
Total Fat	27 g	60 g or less (F), 70 g or less (M)	
Saturated fat	7 g	20 g or less (F), 23 g or less (M)	
Cholesterol	154 mg	300 mg or less	
Sodium	417 mg	2,400 mg or less	
Carbohydrates	1 g	250 g or more	
Protein	48 g	55 g to 90 g	

MARINADE MAGIC

For guaranteeing moist and tender chicken, nothing beats a marinade. The oil or butter keeps the bird juicy, the acid—lemon juice, wine, or vinegar—tenderizes by breaking down the muscle fibers, for tenderness and the herbs and spices provide great flavor.

• Make sure the chicken is washed and patted dry with paper towels, especially if it's been thawed, so the marinade stays full strength and is not diluted.

• Always marinate chicken in a shallow, non-aluminum pan or glass bowl.

• You can also toss chicken and marinade ingredients in a large heavy plastic storage bag; seal tightly and place in a bowl.

• Marinate chicken up to 1 hour at room temperature, then refrigerate up to 24 hours, turning occasionally.

• Drain off the marinade before cooking and use any extra marinade for basting, if desired. If you would like to serve any extra marinade as a sauce, be sure to bring it to a full boil before serving.

FIRECRACKER BBQ CHICKEN

This chicken is fabulous and it's red hot! Using both the microwave and the grill makes for a juicier, faster-cooking bird. *Also pictured on page 130.*

Prep time: 17 minutes plus marinating
Cooking time: 14 minutes
O *Degree of difficulty: easy*

4 teaspoons dry mustard
4 teaspoons chili powder
2 teaspoons minced garlic
1 teaspoon red pepper flakes
1 teaspoon freshly ground pepper
½ teaspoon salt
1 chicken (3 to 3½ pounds), cut up
⅓ cup chili sauce

1 Combine the mustard, chili powder, garlic, red and black peppers, and salt in a small bowl. Rub over the chicken and under the skin. Place chicken in a 13x9-inch microwave-proof dish; cover and refrigerate for 4 hours or overnight.

2 Prepare grill for direct heat or preheat broiler. Grill is ready when white ash forms. Meanwhile, cover chicken with wax paper and microwave on high (100% power) for 10 minutes, rotating the dish halfway through. Reserve the drippings from the pan.

3 Immediately grill or broil chicken about 10 minutes, turning once, until juices run clear when chicken is pierced with a fork.

4 Meanwhile, pour reserved chicken drippings into a 2-cup microwave-proof measure. Stir in the chili sauce. Microwave on high (100% power) about 2 minutes or until boiling; stir. Microwave on high (100% power) for 2 minutes more, stirring again halfway through. Serve with chicken. Makes 4 servings.

PER SERVING		DAILY GOAL
Calories	626	2,000 (F), 2,500 (M)
Total Fat	41 g	60 g or less (F), 70 g or less (M)
Saturated fat	11 g	20 g or less (F), 23 g or less (M)
Cholesterol	203 mg	300 mg or less
Sodium	790 mg	2,400 mg or less
Carbohydrates	8 g	250 g or more
Protein	52 g	55 g to 90 g

NOTES

MEDITERRANEAN GRILLED CHICKEN

Simply delicious! Juniper berries, fresh rosemary, and sage leaves give this dish an authentic taste of the Mediterranean.

Prep time: 15 minutes plus marinating
Cooking time: 30 to 40 minutes
○ *Degree of difficulty: easy*

½ **cup fresh lemon juice**
2 **tablespoons olive oil**
8 **juniper berries, crushed**
1 **tablespoon chopped fresh rosemary**
1 **tablespoon minced garlic**
¾ **teaspoon salt**
¾ **teaspoon freshly ground pepper**
12 **fresh sage leaves**
3 **small chickens (2¼ to 2½ pounds each), split**
2 **fresh rosemary sprigs**

1 For marinade, whisk lemon juice, oil, juniper berries, rosemary, garlic, salt, and pepper together in a 13x9-inch dish.

2 Tuck the sage under the skin of each chicken. Add the chicken and rosemary sprigs to marinade; toss to coat. Cover and refrigerate for 4 hours or overnight.

3 Remove chicken from marinade; sprinkle with more salt and pepper.

4 Prepare grill for indirect heat. Place a disposable foil roasting pan in the bottom center of grill. Arrange 20 charcoal briquettes on each of 2 opposite sides of foil pan. Ignite charcoal.

5 When white ash has formed, grill chicken over medium coals about 30 to 40 minutes, turning every 10 minutes, until juices run clear when chicken is pierced with a fork. Makes 6 servings.

To broil: Preheat broiler and broiler pan. Broil 4 inches from heat source about 30 to 40 minutes, turning as directed for grilling.

PER SERVING		DAILY GOAL
Calories	595	2,000 (F), 2,500 (M)
Total Fat	35 g	60 g or less (F), 70 g or less (M)
Saturated fat	9 g	20 g or less (F), 23 g or less (M)
Cholesterol	209 mg	300 mg or less
Sodium	334 mg	2,400 mg or less
Carbohydrates	2 g	250 g or more
Protein	65 g	55 g to 90 g

NOTES

LEMON GRILLED CHICKEN

Here's a simple fresh herb marinade, which can easily be doubled for any large gathering of friends. To enhance the flavor of the chicken meat, slash the skin so the marinade can penetrate.

Prep time: 30 minutes plus marinating
Grilling time: 25 to 30 minutes
○ *Degree of difficulty: easy*

1	**tablespoon grated lemon peel**
⅓	**cup fresh lemon juice**
¼	**cup olive oil**
¼	**cup chopped fresh parsley**
2	**tablespoons minced shallot**
1	**tablespoon minced garlic**
1	**teaspoon chopped fresh thyme**
½	**teaspoon salt**
¼	**teaspoon freshly ground pepper**
3	**whole chickens (3 pounds each), quartered**

1 For marinade, combine the lemon peel, lemon juice, oil, parsley, shallot, garlic, thyme, salt, and pepper in a large bowl. Dip the chicken in marinade; place in 3 heavy-duty plastic storage bag with any remaining marinade. Seal.

2 Refrigerate for 4 hours. (Can be made ahead. Refrigerate up to 24 hours. Remove from refrigerator 1 hour before grilling.)

3 Prepare grill for indirect heat. Place a disposable foil roasting pan in the bottom center of grill. Arrange 20 charcoal briquettes on each of 2 opposite sides of foil pan. Ignite charcoal.

4 When white ash has formed, grill chicken over medium-low coals about 25 to 35 minutes, turning and brushing with reserved marinade every 5 minutes, until juices run clear when chicken is pierced with a fork. Makes 12 servings.

To broil: Preheat broiler and broiler pan. Broil 4 inches from heat source about 25 to 30 minutes, basting pieces with marinade and turning as directed for grilling.

PER SERVING		DAILY GOAL
Calories	405	2,000 (F), 2,500 (M)
Total Fat	25 g	60 g or less (F), 70 g or less (M)
Saturated fat	6 g	20 g or less (F), 23 g or less (M)
Cholesterol	132 mg	300 mg or less
Sodium	215 mg	2,400 mg or less
Carbohydrates	1 g	250 g or more
Protein	41 g	55 g to 90 g

137

TANGY GRILLED CHICKEN

Packed with zesty flavor, this chicken grills to a nice golden brown and never becomes too dark because there's no sugar in the marinade.

Prep time: 10 minutes plus marinating
Grilling time: 30 to 35 minutes
○ *Degree of difficulty: easy*

2 cups cider vinegar, divided
¼ chopped fresh sage *or* 1 tablespoon dried
1 tablespoon minced garlic
1 tablespoon poultry seasoning
1 large egg
¾ cup vegetable oil
2 tablespoons salt
½ teaspoon freshly ground pepper
2 chickens (3 to 3½ pounds each), quartered

1 For marinade, combine ½ cup of the vinegar, sage, garlic, and poultry seasoning in a small saucepan. Bring to a boil over high heat. Cool to room temperature.

2 Meanwhile, beat the egg in a large bowl. Gradually whisk in the oil, salt, and pepper. Then whisk in the remaining 1½ cups vinegar and the cooled vinegar mixture.

3 Add the chicken to marinade, tossing to coat. Cover and refrigerate for 3 to 4 hours.

4 Remove chicken from refrigerator 30 minutes before grilling.

5 Prepare grill for indirect heat. Place a disposable foil roasting pan in the bottom center of grill. Arrange 20 charcoal briquettes on each of 2 opposite sides of foil pan. Ignite charcoal.

6 When white ash has formed, remove chicken from marinade and grill over medium-low coals about 30 to 35 minutes, turning occasionally, until juices run clear when chicken is pierced with a fork. Makes 8 servings.

PER SERVING		DAILY GOAL
Calories	490	2,000 (F), 2,500 (M)
Total Fat	32 g	60 g or less (F), 70 g or less (M)
Saturated fat	8 g	20 g or less (F), 23 g or less (M)
Cholesterol	156 mg	300 mg or less
Sodium	961 mg	2,400 mg or less
Carbohydrates	2 g	250 g or more
Protein	45 g	55 g to 90 g

NOTES

LEAN 'N' TASTY BARBEQUED CHICKEN

Stay close to the grill when you're cooking this because boneless chicken breasts or thighs cook faster than bone-in chicken. Make the sauce ahead to give the flavors a chance to mellow.

▼ *Low-fat*
▽ *Low -calorie*
   Prep time: 35 minutes plus marinating
   Cooking time: 12 to 14 minutes
↻ *Degree of difficulty: easy*

2 **teaspoons cumin**
1 **teaspoon paprika**
1 **teaspoon dry mustard**
¼ **teaspoon freshly ground pepper**
⅛ **to ¼ teaspoon ground red pepper**
8 **boneless, skinless breast halves** *or*
   thighs (about 2 pounds)
   Salt

Barbeque Sauce
1 **tablespoon vegetable oil**
1 **cup chopped onions**
1 **tablespoon minced garlic**
1 **tablespoon chili powder**
½ **cup ketchup**
½ **cup strong brewed coffee**
¼ **cup Worcestershire sauce**
¼ **cup cider vinegar**
¼ **cup firmly packed brown sugar**
½ **teaspoon salt**

1 Combine cumin, paprika, mustard, and peppers in a cup. Place the chicken in a large glass bowl and rub all over with cumin mixture. Cover and refrigerate 1 hour. (Can be made ahead. Cover and refrigerate up to 24 hours.)

2 Prepare grill for direct heat. Sprinkle chicken pieces lightly with salt. Brush one side with ½ cup of the Barbeque Sauce.

3 When white ash has formed, place pieces, brushed side down, 5 inches from heat and grill over medium coals for 7 minutes. Brush another ½ cup Barbeque Sauce over chicken. Turn chicken over and grill for 5 to 7 minutes more, turning occasionally and basting with more sauce if desired. Makes 8 servings.

To broil: Preheat broiler. Place chicken on a foil-lined broiler pan and broil 3 to 4 inches from heat 10 to 16 minutes, basting pieces with sauce and turning as directed for grilling.

Barbeque Sauce: Heat the oil in medium saucepan over medium-high heat. Add the onions and cook until translucent, about 2 minutes. Add the garlic and chili powder; cook 1 minute more. Stir in ketchup, coffee, Worcestershire sauce, vinegar, brown sugar, and salt. Bring to a boil, reduce heat and simmer 20 minutes, until slightly thickened. Cool. (Can be made ahead. Cover and refrigerate up to one week.) Makes 1⅔ cups.

PER SERVING		DAILY GOAL
Calories	195	2,000 (F), 2,500 (M)
Total Fat	3 g	60 g or less (F), 70 g or less (M)
Saturated fat	1 g	20 g or less (F), 23 g or less (M)
Cholesterol	58 mg	300 mg or less
Sodium	477 mg	2,400 mg or less
Carbohydrates	16 g	250 g or more
Protein	24 g	55 g to 90 g

CARIBBEAN GRILLED CHICKEN

If you're daring, try hot curry powder in this dry spice rub for an extra flavor boost. Serve the chicken with lime wedges.

Prep time: 15 minutes plus marinating
Grilling time: 25 to 35 minutes
○ *Degree of difficulty: easy*

3 **tablespoons curry powder**
1 **tablespoon minced garlic**
2 **teaspoons fresh ginger**
½ **teaspoon salt**
½ **teaspoon allspice**
¼ **teaspoon ground red pepper**
1 **chicken (3½ pounds), cut up**

1 Combine the curry powder, garlic, ginger, salt, allspice, and red pepper in a small bowl. Spread the chicken with rub all over and under skin. Wrap and refrigerate overnight. Remove from refrigerator 1 hour before grilling.

2 Prepare grill for indirect heat. Place disposable foil roasting pan in the bottom center of grill. Open all grill vents. Arrange 20 charcoal briquettes on each of 2 opposite sides of a foil pan. Ignite charcoal.

3 When white ash has formed, grill chicken covered over medium-low coals about 25 to 35 minutes, turning every 5 minutes, until juices run clear when chicken is pierced with a fork. Makes 4 servings.

PER SERVING		DAILY GOAL	
Calories	440	2,000 (F), 2,500 (M)	
Total Fat	24 g	60 g or less (F), 70 g or less (M)	
Saturated fat	7 g	20 g or less (F), 23 g or less (M)	
Cholesterol	154 mg	300 mg or less	
Sodium	420 mg	2,400 mg or less	
Carbohydrates	4 g	250 g or more	
Protein	49 g	55 g to 90 g	

GREAT GRILLING: GET READY BEFORE YOUR BIRD HITS THE FLAME

The secret to perfect grilling is easy— relax and take your time. Whether your chicken is marinated, basted, rubbed with herbs and spices, or simply cooked with no sauce at all, preparing your grill is best done best at a leisurely pace. Here's how:

1 To prepare the grill for direct heat, place the coals in a single layer. Position the rack 5 to 8 inches above coals. Light the charcoal briquettes at least 30 minutes before cooking. They are ready when they are covered with a white ash. Place the chicken on the grill, skin side up with smaller pieces near the edges. Turn chicken often during cooking with long-handled tongs (every 5 to 10 minutes depending on the size of the pieces) for even doneness and charring.

Chicken is done when a fork is inserted easily and the juices run clear.

2 To prepare the grill for indirect heat, place a disposable foil roasting pan in the bottom center of grill. Open all grill vents. Arrange 20 charcoal briquettes on each of 2 opposite sides of a foil pan. Ignite charcoal. When a white ash has formed on the briquettes, place chicken over the drip pan. Cover grill and cook chicken according to recipes.

GRILLED LIME CHICKEN WITH CILANTRO BUTTER

There's no need to marinate this chicken, which is bursting with citrus flavor. It's ready to cook in just the time it takes to heat up the grill.

▽ *Low-calorie*
Prep time: 30 minutes
Cooking time: 20 to 30 minutes
○ *Degree of difficulty: easy*

 1 **tablespoon chopped garlic**
 1 **teaspoon salt**
 ½ **teaspoon freshly ground pepper**
 1 **tablespoon grated lime peel**
 3 **small chickens (2½ to 3 pounds each), cut up**
24 **large sprigs fresh cilantro**
 ¾ **cup butter *or* margarine, melted**
 6 **tablespoons olive oil**
 6 **tablespoons chopped fresh cilantro**

1 Mash the garlic, 1 teaspoon salt, and ½ teaspoon pepper to a paste with a mortar and pestle or the flat side of a large knife on a cutting board. Combine with the lime peel. Spread under skin of each chicken piece; tuck in the cilantro sprigs. (Can be made ahead. Cover and refrigerate up to 24 hours.)

2 Sprinkle the chicken with salt and pepper. Combine the butter, oil, and chopped cilantro in a small bowl. Brush some lightly on chicken.

3 Prepare grill for direct heat. When white ash has formed, grill chicken over medium-hot coals about 20 to 30 minutes, turning every 10 minutes and brushing with additional cilantro butter, until juices run clear when the chicken is pierced with a fork. Makes 12 servings.

To broil: Preheat broiler. Broil 4 inches from heat source about 20 to 30 minutes, turning and brushing with cilantro butter as directed for grilling.

PER SERVING		DAILY GOAL	
Calories	245	2,000 (F), 2,500 (M)	
Total Fat	18 g	60 g or less (F), 70 g or less (M)	
Saturated fat	7 g	20 g or less (F), 23 g or less (M)	
Cholesterol	76 mg	300 mg or less	
Sodium	207 mg	2,400 mg or less	
Carbohydrates	0 g	250 g or more	
Protein	19 g	55 g to 90 g	

A-B

Arroz Con Pollo, 69
Baked Sesame Chicken with Ginger, 115
Balsamic Chicken Breasts, 96
Barbeque Sauce, 139
Batter-Dipped Chicken Nuggets with Sweet-and-Sour
    Orange Sauce, 109
Biscuits, 9
Bistro Roasted Chicken, 56
Black Bean Salad, 66
Blue Cheese
    Blue Cheese Dip, 8
    Buffalo Chicken Wings, 8
    Warm Chicken and Blue Cheese Salad with Walnuts, 122
Brazilian Chicken with Fruit, 37
Brunswick Stew, 14
Buffalo Chicken Wings, 8
Buttermilk Fried Chicken with Pan Gravy, 12

C

Cajun Chicken Sandwich, 102
Caribbean Grilled Chicken, 140
Cheat-the-Clock Cassoulet, 83
Chicken Adobo, 92
Chicken Parmesan Pronto, 82
Chicken Satay with Spicy Peanut Sauce, 30
Chicken á la King, 12-13
Chicken with Caper Cream, 33
Chicken Marsala, 53
Chicken Rolls with Mushrooms and Cream, 17
Chicken and Cornmeal Dumplings, 10
Chicken Jambalaya, 18
Chicken Madeira with Prosciutto, 86
Chicken Orient Express, 93
Chicken Paprikash, 33
Chicken Palermo with Sweet Sausage, 50
Chicken Tonnato Salad, 121
Chicken Normandy, 61
Chicken Waldorf Salad, 129
Chicken Tamales, 73
Chicken Couscous, 34
Chicken Alla Panna Rosa, 52
Chicken Sauté Provençal, 58
Chicken Hacked Chicken, 42
Chicken Burgers with Cranberry Mayonnaise, 103
Chicken Curry in a Hurry, 98

Chicken with Pancetta and Zinfandel, 59
Chicken and Tortilla Soup, 70
Chicken Cacciatore, 56
Chicken Caesar Salad, 120
Chinese Chicken Noodle Soup, 45
Chinese Chicken and Noodles, 126
Chutney
    Country Captain, 13
    Madras Chicken Curry in Spicy Puffs, 36
    Tropical Chicken with Brown Rice, 94
Citrus Chicken Stir-Fry with Spring Vegetables, 44
Classic Chicken Potpie, 16
Coconut/coconut milk
    Brazilian Chicken with Fruit, 37
    Chicken Satay with Spicy Peanut Sauce, 30
    Madras Chicken Curry in Spicy Puffs, 36
    Spicy Peanut Sauce, 30
Cornflake Crunch Chicken, 115
Country Captain, 13
Creamy Cilantro Dressing, 66
Creamy Cilantro Sauce, 127
Creole Tomato Sauce, 18
Crispy Chicken Scaloppine, 117
Curried Lentil Salad with Chicken, 127
Curry Mixture, 13

D-G

Down-Home Chicken and Biscuits, 9
Dumplings, 10
Firecracker BBQ Chicken, 135
Five-Spice Chicken, 41
Fruit
    Brazilian Chicken with Fruit, 37
    Chicken Adobo, 92
    Chicken Curry in a Hurry, 98
    Chicken Normandy, 61
    Grilled Chicken Salad with Summer Fruit, 125
    Sunday's Roasted Chicken with Bulgur Stuffing, 24
Garlicky Chicken Wings, 97
Greek Chicken and Herbed Feta Rolls, 91
Grains/bulgur
    Chicken Couscous, 34
    Roast Herb Chicken with Barley Stuffing, 23
    Sunday's Roasted Chicken with Bulgur Stuffing, 24
Grilled Chicken Fajitas, 65
Grilled Chicken Salad with Summer Fruit, 125
Grilled Lime Chicken with Cilantro Butter, 141

Grilled Provençal Chicken, 132
Grilled Chicken and Spinach Salad, 124
Guacamole, 65

H-L

Ham/prosciutto/sausage
    Cheat-the-Clock Cassoulet, 83
    Chicken Jambalaya, 18
    Chicken Madeira with Prosciutto, 86
    Chicken Palermo with Sweet Sausage, 50
    Chicken with Pancetta and Zinfandel, 59
    Crispy Chicken Scaloppine, 117
    Grilled Chicken and Spinach Salad, 124
    Hot Bacon Dressing, 124
    Prosciutto-Wrapped Chicken with Sage, 51
    Spring Chicken and Asparagus Bundles, 89
    Warm Chicken and Blue Cheese Salad with Walnuts, 122
Hot 'n' Healthy Chicken Enchiladas, 68
Jamaican Jerk Chicken, 29
Japanese Chicken Wings, 40
Lean 'n' Tasty Barbequed Chicken, 139
Lemon Grilled Chicken, 137
Louisiana Chicken and Shrimp Gumbo, 19

M-Q

Madras Chicken Curry in Spicy Puffs, 36
Mediterranean Grilled Chicken, 136
Mexican Chicken Lime Stew, 71
Moroccan Chicken Cutlets, 100
Mushrooms
    Chicken á la King, 12
    Chicken Cacciatore, 56
    Chicken Parmesan Pronto, 82
    Chicken Rolls with Mushrooms and Cream, 17
    Chinese Chicken Noodle Soup, 45
    Roast Herb Chicken with Barley Stuffing, 23
    Stuffed Chicken Breasts Florentine, 55
New Orleans Pecan Chicken, 108
Orange Sauce, 109
Oven-Fried Chicken Bombay, 114
Pacific Rim Chicken Pockets, 48
Pasta
    Chicken Orient Express, 93
    Chinese Chicken and Noodles, 126
    Chinese Chicken Noodle Soup, 45

(Pasta continuied)
    Chinese Hacked Chicken, 42
    Sesame Wheat Noodles, 93
    Spicy Chicken Alfredo, 84
Pistachio Chicken Cutlets, 113
Polenta with Parmesan and Walnuts, 87
Prosciutto Wrapped Chicken with Sage, 51
Quick Chicken Burritos, 64

R-S

Relleno Stuffed Chicken with Black Beans and Creamy
    Cilantro Dressing, 66
Rice
    Chicken Adobo, 92
    Chicken Curry in a Hurry, 98
    Chicken Jambalaya, 18
    Mexican Chicken Lime Stew, 71
    Moroccan Chicken Cutlets, 100
    Oven-Fried Chicken Bombay, 114
    Thai Chicken with Vegetables, 39
    Tropical Chicken with Brown Rice, 94
Roast Herb Chicken with Polenta, 86
Roast Chicken with 20 Cloves of Garlic, 21
Roast Herb Chicken with Barley Stuffing, 23
Roasted Chicken with Cilantro, 74
Roasted Mint Chicken, 22
Salsa Cruda, 65
Sandwiches
    Cajun Chicken Sandwich, 102
    Chicken Burgers with Cranberry Mayonnaise, 103
    Santa Fe Chicken Club Sandwich, 77
    Southwest Chicken Burgers, 79
    Warm Chicken and Pesto Vegetable Sandwich, 105
Santa Fe Chicken Club Sandwich, 77
Sicilian Grilled with Watercress, 88
Skillet Chicken Olé, 70
Southern Buttermilk Chicken, 112
Southwest Chicken Burgers, 79
Spicy Tomato Sauce, 68
Spicy Chicken Alfredo, 84
Spicy Puffs, 36
Spring Chicken and Asparagus Bundles, 89
Soups/stews
    Brunswick Stew, 14
    Cheat-the-Clock Cassoulet, 83
    Chicken and Tortilla Soup, 70
    Chinese Chicken Noodle Soup, 45

    Louisiana Chicken and Shrimp Gumbo, 19
    Mexican Chicken Lime Stew, 71
Stir-Fry Lime Chicken, 47
Stuffed Chicken Breasts Florentine, 55
Sunday's Roasted Chicken with Bulgur Stuffing, 24
Super Crunch Batter-Fried Chicken, 110

T-V

Tandoori Chicken, 28
Tangy Grilled Chicken, 138
Tex-Mex Chicken, 75
Texas Heat Wave Chicken Wings, 76
Thai Chicken with Vegetables, 39
Tomatoes/tomato sauce
    Arroz Con Pollo, 69
    Brunswick Stew, 14
    Chicken Alla Panna Rosa, 52
    Chicken Cacciatore, 56
    Chicken Couscous, 34
    Chicken Sauté Provençal, 58
    Chicken Tonnato Salad, 121
    Country Captain, 13
    Hot 'n' Healthy Chicken Enchiladas, 68
    Jamaican Jerk Chicken, 29
    Mexican Chicken Lime Stew, 71
    Quick Chicken Burritos, 64
    Relleno-Stuffed Chicken with Black Beans and Creamy
        Cilantro Dressing, 66
    Spicy Tomato Sauce, 68
Tonnato Dressing, 121
Tropical Chicken with Brown Rice, 94
Vegetables
    Brunswick Stew, 14
    Chicken á la King, 12
    Chicken Adobo, 92
    Chicken and Cornmeal Dumplings, 10
    Chicken and Tortilla Soup, 70
    Chicken Cacciatore, 56
    Chicken Couscous, 34
    Chicken Curry in a Hurry, 98
    Chicken Orient Express, 93
    Chicken Tamales, 73
    Chicken Tonnato Salad, 121
    Chinese Chicken Noodle Soup, 45
    Classic Chicken Potpie, 16
    Country Captain, 13
    Down-Home Chicken and Biscuits, 9

Greek Chicken and Herbed Feta Rolls, 91
Madras Chicken Curry in Spicy Puffs, 36
Mexican Chicken Lime Stew, 71
Moroccan Chicken Cutlets, 100
Pacific Rim Chicken Pockets, 48
Spring Chicken and Asparagus Bundles, 89
Stir-Fry Lime Chicken, 47
Stuffed Chicken Breasts Florentine, 55
Sunday's Roasted Chicken with Bulgar Stuffing, 24
Thai Chicken with Vegetables, 39
Warm Chicken and Pesto Vegetable Sandwich, 105
Vietnamese Chicken Bundles, 46

W-Z

Warm Chicken and Pesto Vegetable Sandwich, 105
Warm Chicken Salad with Goat Cheese, 129
Warm Chicken and Blue Cheese Salad with Walnuts, 122
Watercress
    Citrus Chicken Stir-Fry with Spring Vegetables, 44
    Grilled Chicken Salad with Summer Fruit, 125
    Sicilian Grilled Chicken with Watercress, 88
Yogurt/sour cream/buttermilk
    Chicken Paprikash, 33
    Creamy Cilantro Dressing, 66
    Creamy Cilantro Sauce, 127
    New Orleans Pecan Chicken, 108
    Southern Buttermilk Chicken, 112
    Southwest Chicken Burgers, 79
    Super Crunch Batter-Fried Chicken, 110
    Tandoori Chicken, 28
    Yogurt Sauce, 114

Tips

A Carving Primer, 57
A Guide to the Perfect Fried Chicken, 112-113
Any Way You Cut It, 101
Hot 'n' Healthy Chicken, 32
How Much to Buy, 37
Marinade Magic, 132
Perfect Chicken Cutlets, 117
Poultry Hotline, 17
The Perfect Roast, 22
The Simplest Chicken Broth, 40

METRIC COOKING HINTS

By making a few conversions, cooks in Australia, Canada, and the United Kingdom can use the recipes in Ladies' Home Journal® *100 Great Chicken Recipes* with confidence. The charts on this page provide a guide for converting measurements from the U.S. customary system, which is used throughout this book, to the imperial and metric systems. There also is a conversion table for oven temperatures to accommodate the differences in oven calibrations.

Volume and Weight: Americans traditionally use cup measures for liquid and solid ingredients. The chart (top right) shows the approximate imperial and metric equivalents. If you are accustomed to weighing solid ingredients, here are some helpful approximate equivalents.
- 1 cup butter, castor sugar, or rice = 8 ounces = about 250 grams
- 1 cup flour = 4 ounces = about 125 grams
- 1 cup icing sugar = 5 ounces = about 150 grams

Spoon measures are used for smaller amounts of ingredients. Although the size of the tablespoon varies slightly among countries. However, for practical purposes and for recipes in this book, a straight substitution is all that's necessary.

Measurements made using cups or spoons should always be level, unless stated otherwise.

Product Differences: Most of the ingredients called for in the recipes in this book are available in English-speaking countries. However, some are known by different names. Here are some common American ingredients and their possible counterparts:
- Sugar is granulated or castor sugar.
- Powdered sugar is icing sugar.
- All-purpose flour is plain household flour or white flour. When self-rising flour is used in place of all-purpose flour in a recipe that calls for leavening, omit the leavening agent (baking soda or baking powder) and salt.
- Light corn syrup is golden syrup.
- Cornstarch is cornflour.
- Baking soda is bicarbonate of soda.
- Vanilla is vanilla essence.

USEFUL EQUIVALENTS

⅛ teaspoon = 0.5ml
¼ teaspoon = 1ml
½ teaspoon = 2 ml
1 teaspoon = 5 ml
¼ cup = 2 fluid ounces = 50ml
⅓ cup = 3 fluid ounces = 75ml
½ cup = 4 fluid ounces = 125ml

⅔ cup = 5 fluid ounces = 150ml
¾ cup = 6 fluid ounces = 175ml
1 cup = 8 fluid ounces = 250ml
2 cups = 1 pint
2 pints = 1 litre
½ inch =1 centimetre
1 inch = 2 centimetres

BAKING PAN SIZES

American	Metric
8x1½-inch round baking pan	20x4-centimetre sandwich or cake tin
9x1½-inch round baking pan	23x3.5-centimetre sandwich or cake tin
11x7x1½-inch baking pan	28x18x4-centimetre baking pan
13x9x2-inch baking pan	32.5x23x5-centimetre baking pan
2-quart rectangular baking dish	30x19x5-centimetre baking pan
15x10x2-inch baking pan	38x25.5x2.5-centimetre baking pan (Swiss roll tin)
9-inch pie plate	22x4- or 23x4-centimetre pie plate
7- or 8-inch springform pan	18- or 20-centimetre springform or loose-bottom cake tin
9x5x3-inch loaf pan	23x13x6-centimetre or 2-pound narrow loaf pan or paté tin
1½-quart casserole	1.5-litre casserole
2-quart casserole	2-litre casserole

OVEN TEMPERATURE EQUIVALENTS

Farenheit Setting	Celsius Setting*	Gas Setting
300°F	150°C	Gas Mark 2
325°F	160°C	Gas Mark 3
350°F	180°C	Gas Mark 4
375°F	190°C	Gas Mark 5
400°F	200°C	Gas Mark 6
425°F	220°C	Gas Mark 7
450°F	230°C	Gas Mark 8
Broil		Grill

Electric and gas ovens may be calibrated using Celsius. However, increase the Celsius setting 10 to 20 degrees when cooking above 160°C with an electric oven. For convection or forced-air ovens (gas or electric), lower the temperature setting 10°C when cooking at all heat levels.